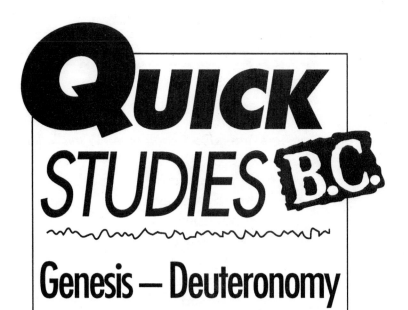

QUICK STUDIES B.C.
Genesis — Deuteronomy

DAVID C. COOK PUBLISHING CO.
ELGIN, ILLINOIS—PARIS, ONTARIO

The following authors and editors contributed to this volume:

Stan Campbell
Karen Dockrey
Randy Southern
Kevin Stirratt
Mark Syswerda
Rick Thompson
Jim Townsend, Ph.D.

Quick Studies B.C.
Genesis—Deuteronomy: The Pentateuch

© 1994 David C. Cook Publishing Co.

Published by David C. Cook Publishing Co.
850 North Grove Ave., Elgin, IL 60120
Cable address: DCCOOK
Designed by Bill Paetzold
Cover illustrations by Mick Coulas
Inside illustrations by Michael Fleishman
Printed in U.S.A.

ISBN: 0-7814-5157-4

CONTENTS

GENESIS

EXODUS

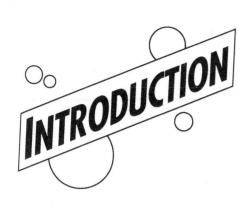

Quick Questions about Quick Studies

We've made *Quick Studies B.C.* as self-explanatory as possible, so you can dive in and start using them right away. But just in case you were wondering . . .

When should I use *Quick Studies B.C.*?
Whenever you want high school or junior high kids to explore the Bible face-to-face and absorb it into their lives. We've kept the openers active and the discussion questions creative, so you can use *Quick Studies B.C.* with confidence in Sunday school, midweek youth Bible study, small groups, even youth group meetings and retreats.

What's so quick about *Quick Studies B.C.*?
They're designed to save you preparation time. The session plans are compact, for quick reading. There aren't a lot of materials to gather, either (you'll need Bibles, pencils and paper, copies of the reproducible sheets, and sometimes a few other items). Yet *Quick Studies B.C.* are *real* Bible studies, with plenty of thought-provoking discussion and life application.

How are these different from other youth Bible studies?
We like to think *Quick Studies B.C.* are . . .
• *Irresistible.* You already know most kids don't jump at the chance to fill in a bunch of blanks in a boring study guide. So we used creative, reproducible sheets and *active* activities to draw kids into Scripture.
• *Involving.* You need discussion *starters*, not discussion *stoppers*. We avoided dull "yes or no" questions and included lots of thought-provokers that should get your group members talking about important issues. And we didn't forget suggested *answers* to most of the tougher questions, which should make things easier for you.
• *Inductive.* Many Bible studies try to force-feed kids a single "aim" and ignore other points Scripture is trying to make. *Quick Studies B.C.* let kids discover a variety of key principles in a passage.
• *Influential.* It's not enough to know what the Bible says. Every session includes a step designed to help kids decide what to do *personally* with vital points from the passage.

When do kids read the passages covered?
That's up to you. If your group is into homework, assign the passages in advance. If not, take time to read the Scripture together after the "Opening Act" step that kicks off each session. There are dozens of ways to read a passage—with volunteers taking turns, or with a narrator and actors "performing" a scene, or with kids underlining points as they read silently, or with you reading as the author and kids listening as the original audience, or with small groups paraphrasing as they read . . .

What if I want to cover more—or less—than a chapter in a session?
Quick Studies B.C. are flexible. Each 45- to 60-minute session covers a chapter of the Old Testament, but you can adjust the speed to fit your group. To cover more than one passage in a session, just pick the points you want to emphasize and drop the activities, questions, and reproducible sheets you don't need. To cover less than a chapter, you may need to add a few questions and spend more time discussing the "So What?" application step in detail.

Do I have to cover a whole Old Testament book?
No. Each session stands alone. Use sessions one at a time if you want to, or mix and match books in any order you choose. No matter how you use them, *Quick Studies B.C.* are likely to help your group see Bible study in a whole new light.

Randy Southern, Series Editor

GENESIS 1–2

Something from Nothing

OVERVIEW

God creates a perfect, sinless world and fills it with a wide variety of plants and animals. Then He creates a man and a woman to live in the Garden of Eden and oversee it. Everything God makes is good.

OPENING ACT

(Needed: Craft materials [optional])

Hand out paper and pencils. Ask group members to invent something that no one has ever thought of—and to be ready to explain exactly how it should work. (If you have modeling clay or similar craft materials, you might have group members build three-dimensional versions of their inventions.) Their "inventions" may include plants, animals, mechanical devices, or whatever. After group members show and explain (or demonstrate) their creations, point out how much of what they created is based on other things they are familiar with. Have them consider how much more difficult it would be to create something if they had to start completely "from scratch." (For example, think what would be required to create a primary color that doesn't yet exist.)

DATE I USED THIS SESSION _____ GROUP I USED IT WITH _____

NOTES FOR NEXT TIME _____

_____

_____

Q&A

1. **Do you have something at home that you've created—like a poem, story, model, song, drawing, or painting—that you're proud of? If so, describe it. Then explain why you're happy about having done it.** After kids answer, explain that creativity is one way we imitate (and honor) our Creator.

2. **We get a good idea in Genesis 1 of *how* God created the earth. But *why* do you think He created it?** (Perhaps simply because He knew it would be "good.") If no one mentions it, point out that God also has given us the special privilege of being allowed to interact with Him.

3. **Do you think the "days" of creation were twenty-four-hour periods? Why?** (Opinions may vary, but since the sun was not created until Day 4, some people find it hard to be strict about a twenty-four-hour-day argument.)

4. **You may notice that the phrase "according to their kind" is used frequently** (1:11, 12, 21, 24, 25). **Do you think the phrase is important? If so, why?** (It has become the basis of a biblical defense against evolution theories. While there is fossil evidence showing development [or "evolution"] within kinds, there is still insufficient evidence for crossover between kinds. The horse is an evolution "of its kind." Mankind and other primates are different kinds.)

5. **Why do you think God created such a variety of plants and animals? Couldn't He have gotten by with one or two species so we could just have something to eat?** (God's greatness is certainly reflected in His creation. Not only do we have a vast variety of food choices, but we also can marvel at the many kinds of birds, animals, and insects everywhere we look—beneath the sea, on the polar ice caps, underground, deep in the jungles, in the hottest deserts, and so forth.)

6. **In Genesis 1:26, why do you think God says, "Let *us* make man in *our* image"** (italics added)**?** (Even from the creation of the world, we get a hint of how the persons of the Godhead [the Trinity—God the Father, Christ the Son, and the Holy Spirit] operate as one, single God.)

7. What do you think it means to be created "in the image of God" (1:27)? **When you look in a mirror, do you see godly features looking back at you?** (God is Spirit, and is not limited to human form. To be created "in His image" means that we are capable of reflecting His nature and characteristics, such as love, truth, wisdom, and so forth.)

8. When you read the story of the creation of man and woman (2:7; 21-25), **how does it make you feel in contrast to the theory of evolution that suggests mankind evolved from lower primates?**

9. Almost as soon as God created Adam, He put him to work (2:15-20). **Why do you think God didn't allow Adam to "take it easy"?** (Work is not meant to be a drudgery. Being useful and productive *should* make us feel good.)

10. Does Genesis 2:24 make sense to you? Since Adam and Eve had no parents, why would God place this instruction at this point in the Bible? (All future marriages should reflect the "two becoming one" model of Adam and Eve. When people stray from that model, they usually face problems.)

11. Put yourself in the place of Adam or Eve in the Garden of Eden. Describe how you think you would feel and why.

(Needed: Refreshments)

If possible, let kids go outside to complete the reproducible sheet, "Way to Go, God!" Let them decide what they enjoy—and question—most about God's creation. When they come back inside, have a smorgasbord of food ready for them. Challenge them to take time every day during the next week to thank God specifically for the wide variety of good creations that we so often take for granted.

WAY TO GO, GOD!

On the way to this meeting today, how many species of plants did you pass? How many kinds of animals did you see? What different types of birds flew overhead? How many kinds of bugs did you step over (or on)? If you don't know, you should look closer next time. God created these things for you to enjoy and appreciate. For each of the "days" of creation, write down (1) the thing you most appreciate about whatever He created that day, (2) the strangest thing you can think of about that day's creation, and (3) any questions you have about what was created that day.

	Best Thing	Strangest Thing	Questions
Day 1 Light and darkness			
Day 2 The sky			
Day 3 Land, seas, plants, trees			
Day 4 Sun, moon, individual days			
Day 5 Birds and water creatures			
Day 6 Land creatures, man, woman			

"The heavens declare the glory of God; the skies proclaim the work of His hands" (Psalm 19:1).

GENESIS 3

When Fall Comes to Eden

In spite of God's perfect creation and provision for His people, Adam and Eve are tempted and choose to sin. As a result, they are cast out of the garden, and mankind's relationship with God is drastically affected.

(Needed: Temptation objects)

Create a temptation that is likely to be particularly strong for your group members. One option is to place a small box of marbles upside down on a hard table. (Place a piece of cardboard over the open top and then slide the cardboard out after turning the box upside down. Put a sign on the box that says "If you pick up this box, you'll be sorry." Another option is to put a "Do Not Touch" sign on a platter of cookies that is secretly monitored by a video camera. Make sure the temptation is in a prominent location, and that all adults are out of the room. See how long your group members can withstand the temptation before their curiosity gets the better of them.

DATE I USED THIS SESSION _____ GROUP I USED IT WITH _____

NOTES FOR NEXT TIME _____

_____

_____

1. Of all of the temptations that young people face today—premarital sex, drinking, drugs, lying, gossiping, etc.—which would you say is hardest to resist? Why?

2. God only had one rule for Adam and Eve in the Garden of Eden: Don't eat from one specific tree. Why do you think they were unable to obey one little rule? (Obedience is more an attitude than an exertion of effort. Whether we're trying to obey one rule, ten commandments, or whatever, we must first *want* to obey.)

3. Can you think of temptations today that might be similar to the serpent's promise that "your eyes will be opened" (3:5)? (Drinking to get a "buzz," using drugs, and having sex are said by certain people to be "enlightening" activities.)

4. Why do you think Eve gave in to the serpent's tempting? (For one thing, the fruit appealed to more than one of her senses. It appealed to both sight and taste. The serpent's promise also offered the potential of increased wisdom.)

5. Whose fault was it that Adam ate of the fruit? Explain. (Even though some people try to lay the blame on Eve, it's clear that Adam made a conscious decision to eat the fruit [3:6]. Adam was responsible for his action.)

6. What parts of the serpent's promise came true? (Adam and Eve's eyes were opened, they did have a new [and uncomfortable] awareness of good and evil, and they didn't die physically right away.) **What part didn't come true?** (Adam and Eve didn't become "like God," as they'd hoped.)

7. What were the first, immediate results of Adam and Eve's sin? (They became more distant from each other and from God as well. Sin always leads to separation from God.)

8. How eager were Adam and Eve to confess the truth to God? (Both first hid from Him, and then looked for someone else to blame rather than take responsibility for their own actions.) **Why is it sometimes hard to confess our sins?**

9. God could have just let Adam, Eve, and the serpent die. Then He could have started over with new people. Why do you think He chose to do what He did instead? (Perhaps *anyone* in the same situation would eventually have given in to temptation and sin. It seems that even at this early stage, God had a plan of salvation ready. [See verse 15.])

10. Do you think God was cruel to cast Adam and Eve out of Eden? Why or why not? If no one mentions it, point out that even though God banished humans from the idyllic setting of Eden, He did not turn His back on them completely.

11. What can you learn from Adam and Eve to help you deal with the personal temptations you face?

The reproducible sheet, "Underneath the Glitter," challenges group members to identify the "disguises" of many temptations they might face. If time permits, have kids do impromptu skits based on some of the situations they've identified in which someone tempts them to do something wrong under the guise of "having fun" or some other innocent pretense. Close in prayer, asking God for wisdom to identify temptations that may not be as obvious as others, but are just as dangerous.

underneath the

glitter

We've all heard that "All that glitters is not gold." But to go one step further, we should be aware that "Some things that glitter may be quite dangerous." Think about it. What if someone tempted you to smoke by saying, "Hey, kid, how'd you like to have yellow teeth, awful breath, and a life expectancy that's just a fraction of what it is now?"? Most of us would pass. So instead, we're promised popularity, acceptance, and other things. The effects of smoking are just as deadly, but many people fall for the shallow promises.

For each of the items below, write down how someone might try to convince you to get involved. (If *you* were trying to convince someone to join you in one of these activities, what would be *your* best line?) Then write down the potential consequences of falling for such a line.

Activity . . .	"Glittery" Temptation . . .	Real Results . . .
Smoking	• Show your independence. • Get your own section in restaurants. • Be the first kid on your block to be truly cool	• Lung cancer and other diseases • Disgusting breath • Nicotine addiction
Drinking		
Drug use		
Sexual activity		
Cheating		
Lying to parents		

The Cain Mutiny

It doesn't take long for sin to have an effect on Adam and Eve's family after leaving Eden. In a fit of jealousy, Cain (Adam and Eve's son) kills his younger brother, Abel. Cain is then confronted by God about his act of rage.

Try to evoke some feelings of jealousy in your group members as you begin the session. For example, you might show favoritism to one group over another (girls over guys, kids wearing jeans over kids wearing dressier clothes, etc.). But don't reveal the criteria you're using to make your distinctions. Begin with subtle things such as talking to one group while ignoring the other. Gradually intensify the distinctions. For example, you might let your preferred group have extra refreshments, be excluded from an assignment, or enjoy some similar treatment. After a while, let both groups discuss how they felt. Explain that everyone gets jealous from time to time, but if feelings of jealousy aren't dealt with in a healthy manner, the results can be quite serious.

DATE I USED THIS SESSION _____ GROUP I USED IT WITH _____

NOTES FOR NEXT TIME _____

_____

_____

1. What do you think is the most common cause of jealousy? Why do people get jealous?

2. Do you think Cain was Adam and Eve's first child? (Some people suggest that Eve's judgment of *greatly increased* pain in childbirth [3:16] could indicate previous births. Also, the sudden mention of Cain's wife [4:17] suggests people other than Adam, Eve, Cain, and Abel.)

3. Why do you think God was displeased with Cain's offering (4:4, 5)**? Does He have something against fruits and vegetables?** (Grain offerings would later become part of the Israelites' worship [Leviticus 2], so the problem was not necessarily the offering itself. We get a better clue from I John 3:12, which suggests that God's disfavor was with the *attitude* of Cain—not his offering.)

4. Do you think Cain had a right to be angry because Abel's sacrifice was more acceptable to God? Why? (It seems normal to be upset. If the problem was with Cain's attitude, however, he should have been angry with himself. This might have been the first opportunity for someone to feel anger, but not give in to the urge to sin [Ephesians 4:26].)

5. God tried to deal directly with Cain to settle the matter (4:6, 7)**. Why do you think Cain didn't listen?** (When people allow emotions to overrule reason, they tend to act irresponsibly.)

6. What makes Abel's murder (4:8) **particularly noteworthy?** (It was the first one; it was committed by his brother; it was premeditated; it was in no way deserved; etc.)

7. Do you think Cain really thought he could lie to or fool God (4:9)**? What are some ways people today attempt to do similar things?** (Going to church once a week just for show, expecting it to somehow "cancel out" all of the nasty things we've done during the week; saying the right words during prayer, but lacking true repentance; neglecting to study the Bible and then "pleading ignorance" when we don't do what we're supposed to do; etc.)

8. Cain must have thought he was pretty tough when he was planning and carrying out Abel's murder. But as soon as God began to hold him accountable for his actions, Cain began to whimper and whine. **Do you think he had a right to complain about his punishment? When *you* suffer the consequences of doing something wrong, do you tend to complain? Why?** (Sometimes we're more sorry that we get caught than for what we've done. Perhaps that was true of Cain as well.)

9. **What did Cain lose by killing Abel** (4:10-14)**?** (A brother, fellowship with his parents, a comfortable lifestyle, enjoyment of meeting new people, etc.) **What did he gain?** (Nothing. His act was truly senseless.)

10. **Why do you think God agreed to protect Cain** (4:13-16)**? Don't you think Cain deserved whatever happened to him?** (God had determined Cain's punishment, and that would be enough. God's discipline is for our good, not our harm. We shouldn't be afraid of confessing our sins to Him. We should be more afraid to *not* confess the things we've done.)

11. **What can you learn about jealousy from this story?** (While our feelings may be strong, we should think things through in light of what God wants before acting on them.)

SO WHAT?

The reproducible sheet, "Caught in the Act," contains a number of scenarios. Close by reading the "setup" of each scenario and then having volunteers act it out the rest of the way. Each scenario can be used twice—once in which the person who is caught tries to talk his or her way out of the situation with an excuse or a lie, and a second time in which the person "comes clean" and confesses. Contrast the consequences of confessing with those of denying responsibility. Explain that even when we "get away with" something, we suffer guilt and the fear of being discovered. So if we're going to suffer anyway, it's usually much easier to suffer the consequences of confession rather than trying to lie our way out of uncomfortable situations. Besides, confession is the only way to eliminate *spiritual* problems.

CAUGHT IN THE ACT

How would you respond to each of the following situations?

1. You've been warned repeatedly by your parents that you're expected to be home by midnight. It's not just another stupid rule. Your parents both have to be at work very early in the morning, and they want to be sure you're safely home before they go to sleep. But, as usual, you've hung around with your friends, and before you know it, it's 1:15. When you get home, you discover both of your parents waiting for you. Surprisingly, they look less angry than tired and disappointed. But the first thing you hear is "We think it's time to set some new ground rules—unless, of course, you have a good excuse."

_____

_____

_____

2. You don't know how it got started, but one of the favorite things you and your friends like to do at school is make fun of one particular teacher. He's a nice enough guy, but not the sharpest person you've ever seen. He's short, balding, a little overweight, and seems to have no sense of humor—in other words, a perfect target for your jokes. One day you're doing your imitation of the guy, late to class and waddling as fast as he can to get there. You think it's among your best work, but you notice no one is laughing. You slowly turn to look behind you, and sure enough, there he is. He asks, "What are you doing?"

_____

_____

3. You have a part-time job at a bookstore. As you're being trained by another employee, she whispers that it's OK for employees to take home damaged merchandise. She makes sure no one else is looking, rips the jacket of a $25 book, and says, "Like this one, for instance. Everyone does it. The owner doesn't mind, but we just don't talk about it." It sounds fishy to you. Two weeks later you desperately need a book for a school report, but someone has it checked out of the library. You find a copy in your store and think, _OK. Just this once. What's the difference?_ You take the book to a corner of the store and begin to "accidentally" damage it by dropping it on the floor, trying to bend one of the corners. The store owner (whom you didn't see on the floor of the next aisle, stocking shelves) rushes over and yells, "What do you think you're doing?"

_____

_____

_____

GENESIS 6–9

Looks Like Rain

Since the fall of Adam and Eve, sin and evil have spread throughout the world. In an extreme plan to reduce godlessness and reward the faithful few, God sends a massive flood. Only Noah and his family—the ones who have prepared—are spared, as well as the animal life they are overseeing.

(Needed: Squirt guns, blindfolds)

To introduce a "rainy" theme, divide group members into several teams. Blindfold one person on each team; then hide one squirt gun for each team. (Squirt guns should be designated by number or color, so that only Team #1's volunteer can locate and use Squirt Gun #1.) Spin the blindfolded people to disorient them. At your signal, team members should shout instructions to their volunteers, directing them to the team's squirt gun. When a blindfolded player finds the appropriate squirt gun, he or she may take off the blindfold and use the squirt gun on other blindfolded people until they have all located their weapons. Then reload the squirt guns, call for new volunteers, and play as time allows. (For smaller groups, a couple of volunteers can compete to find a single hidden squirt gun.)

DATE I USED THIS SESSION _____ GROUP I USED IT WITH _____

NOTES FOR NEXT TIME _____

_____

_____

1. How do you feel when you're in a really bad storm? What emotions do storms inspire? Have you ever been at sea or out on a lake when a big storm came up suddenly? If so, what was it like?

2. Some people talk of the great flood and suggest that God must be very cruel to wipe out so many people just because they weren't perfect. Read Genesis 6:5, 6 and tell me if you agree.

3. How do you think Noah felt when God told him His plans for destroying the earth's inhabitants? (Stunned? Relieved that he'd found favor in God's eyes? Sad for the people who would face God's judgment? Overwhelmed by the task at hand?)

4. The Bible doesn't say clearly whether or not Noah warned his neighbors about God's impending judgment—unless II Peter 2:5 is an indication. But if he did, how do you think they might have responded? How do you think they might have responded after the second or third straight day of rain?

5. How long do you think it would take you to gather a male and female of every species of animal on the earth? How long did Noah have (7:2-4)? (Seven days.) How was Noah able to do this (7:8, 9)? (He didn't do it; God did.)

6. What animal(s) would you least like to take a sea voyage with? Why? How do you think Noah felt around those animals? Discuss how we may not always be *eager* to do as God commands, but we should still be obedient.

7. How long was Noah on the ark? This is a trick question. We know it rained forty days and nights, but it took much longer for the waters to recede. Compare the dates in Genesis 7:11 and 8:13, 14 to discover that confinement in the ark lasted for more than a year.

8. How many times did Noah send birds out of the ark? (Four. [See Genesis 8:6-12.]) Why do you think he did that? (After forty days of being stationary [8:6], perhaps

Noah [and probably the animals] were getting a case of "cabin fever" and were eager to get out as soon as possible.)

9. **After so long in confinement, what's the first thing you would do when the door opened? What was one of Noah's first actions (8:20)?** (He built an altar to God.)

10. **After the flood, did Noah "live happily ever after" (9:20-27)? Explain.** (No. He planted vineyards, made wine, got drunk, and passed out naked. Consequently, one of his sons saw him and apparently made fun of him or otherwise showed disrespect. The incident resulted in ongoing family conflict and division.)

11. **What can you learn from the story of Noah to apply to your own life?**

Hand out copies of the reproducible sheet, "Promises, Promises." Explain that a covenant is a promise, usually with some conditions attached that must be fulfilled in order to benefit from the promise. Give kids a few minutes to look up the passages and fill in the information. When everyone is finished, go through the sheet, asking volunteers to share what they wrote. (Genesis 9:8-17—Noah; God promised never again to destroy all earthly life with a flood; the sign of the covenant was a rainbow; Genesis 15:9-21—Abraham; God promised to give Abraham's descendants the land described in verses 18-21; II Samuel 7:5-16—David; God promised that David's descendants would lead Israel to rest in the promised land; Matthew 26:26-29; Hebrews 8:6-13—Everyone; Christ shed His blood for our sins so that our relationship with God may be restored.) Afterward, ask: **What do the Old Testament covenants tell us about God?** (He provides for and protects those who are faithful to Him.) **What does the "New Covenant" tell us about God?** (He loves us so much that He sent His only Son to die for us to restore the relationship between us and Him.) Close in prayer, thanking God for His "New Covenant." After the session, make yourself available to any kids who'd like to talk to you more about the "New Covenant" in Christ.

Promises, Promises

Look up the following passages. Then fill in the details of God's covenants—who received each covenant and what each covenant involved.

Passage	Who Received the Covenant?	What Was Involved in the Covenant?
Genesis 9:8-17		
Genesis 15:9-21		
II Samuel 7:5-16		
Matthew 26:26-29; Hebrews 8:6-13		

GENESIS 11:1-9

Say What?

God's command to "Be fruitful and . . . fill the earth" (9:1) appears to go unheeded. Instead, humankind attempts to unite and accomplish great things without God's help (11:4). When people try to build a tower to the heavens and "make a name" for themselves, God uses a creative method to disperse them.

(Needed: Building materials)

Have kids form teams. Provide each team with an equal amount of building materials (Tinkertoys, Legos, wooden blocks, playing cards, etc.). Explain that the teams will compete in a two-part contest. The first part is to see which team can build the tallest tower. (If you wish, originality can also be made a consideration.) After the teams have assembled their towers, announce the second part of the contest: the support test. Place a brick or some type of heavy object on top of each structure. Determine the tallest tower only *after* the support test. Later, you can use this exercise to point out that the greatest achievements of collective humankind (such as the Tower of Babel) are insignificant compared to God's "weight" and power.

DATE I USED THIS SESSION _____ GROUP I USED IT WITH _____

NOTES FOR NEXT TIME _____

_____

_____

1. What's the most impressive building you've ever seen? Why? What's the tallest building you've ever been in? How does it feel to look down on the rest of the world from a high place?

2. How do you think your life would be different today if "the whole world had one language and a common speech" (11:1)? (Would racism and prejudice be decreased? Would there be one big country instead of many? Would travel be more fun or less fun?)

3. What was the problem with the goal of the people? Didn't God want them to build towers? (Their goal [11:4] suggests a proud attitude and direct defiance of God's previous command to "fill the earth" [9:1].)

4. Genesis 11:5 tells us "the Lord came down" to see what the people were doing. Do you think He felt threatened by the people's efforts? Explain. (Anyone who has been up the Sears Tower or Empire State Building, or who has flown in a plane, knows it's ludicrous to seriously consider building a tower that would rival God's place in the heavens.)

5. Why does God suggest that "nothing they plan to do will be impossible for them" (11:6)? (It's a matter of attitude. Much the same as a parent sets specific boundaries for his or her children, God knew the people shouldn't think they had "gotten away with" this attempt to be godlike.)

6. What else could God could have done to deal with these proud people? (He had dealt with the sinfulness of Noah's time with a severe flood. Obviously, He could have done anything. But this time, He chose a gentler way to handle the problem.)

7. What do you think it might have been like to suddenly be speaking different languages? The skit on the reproducible sheet, "Anguage-Lay Arriers-Bay," should help kids get a sense of what took place. Assign people to read the parts. Then discuss what it might be like if a similar kind of thing happened at their school.

8. Do you think people generally respond better to God when He asks nicely, or when He has to take more drastic steps to get their attention? Why? (Some people tend to ignore God until He gets forceful with them.)

9. How long do you suppose the people tried to communicate with each other in different languages before they gave up and spread out?

10. Suppose you and your friends were getting together to do something you shouldn't. If God wanted to use a creative method to keep it from happening or to put an end to it, what might He do? Emphasize that we need to put an end to such things ourselves—*before* God decides to take the kinds of actions group members have suggested.

Point out that the trouble among the people took place because they were more concerned with talking to *each other* than with talking to *God*. When we communicate with God clearly and regularly, we usually don't experience so many problems communicating with each other. The problem is that we usually communicate with God using silent prayer, in which our thoughts may tend to wander. So rather than closing the session in prayer, you might want to have your group members write individual letters to God instead. They should write out as specifically as possible the things they normally pray for. Their prayers should include praise, confession, thanksgiving, and intercession, as well as personal requests. Have kids take home their written prayers. Challenge them to add to the prayer each day during the next week. Also encourage them to restore any lines of communication with God that may have been recently neglected.

Anguage-Lay Arriers-Bay

(A read-along skit for people who weren't paying attention during the reading of the Bible story.)

NARRATOR: Once upon a time there lived a group of people. They were supposed to spread out over the whole earth, but they decided to just hang around in the same place.

PERSON 1: So, whaddaya wanna do today?

PERSON 2: I don't know. What do you want to do?

PERSON 1: You want to go to the mall?

PERSON 2: Naw. It's too late. Besides, malls haven't been invented yet.

NARRATOR: Then one day something happened that would change their lives forever.

PERSON 1: So whaddaya wanna do today?

PERSON 3: I know. Let's build a tower.

PERSON 4: Huh? Why would we want to do that?

PERSON 3: Because we can work together and build the tallest tower in the world.

PERSON 4: OK. Cool.

PERSON 2: People will be forced to look up to us.

PERSON 1: They'll see us from hundreds of miles away. Oops! Miles haven't been invented yet, either. They'll, uh, see us from thousands of cubits away.

PERSON 3: We'll be the talk of the town.

PERSON 1: We'll be on *Oprah.* . . . I know, I know—

EVERYONE: *Oprah* hasn't been invented yet!

NARRATOR: It was an ambitious project, to be sure, but God was not pleased that the people continued to disobey Him and go about with their own agendas. So He took action.

PERSON 3: We're going to be famous.

PERSON 4: We'll be heroes.

PERSON 2: When we finish this, we'll be like gods!

PERSON 1: Carpe diem!

PERSON 2: Viva la tour!

PERSON 3: La torre es muy grande.

PERSON 4: What did you say? I didn't understand you guys.

PERSON 3: Que? No comprendo!

PERSON 2: Je ne cést pas.

NARRATOR: And from that point on, there was only one thing left to do.

PERSON 4: You guys are too weird for me. I'm outta here!

PERSON 3: Adios senoras y senoritas.

PERSON 1: Auf Wiedersehen.

PERSON 2: Adieu.

NARRATOR: And they all lived a little more confused ever after.

GENESIS 12–15

Pathways and Promises

The language scrambling at the Tower of Babel managed to finally disperse the people, but sin is again prominent throughout the world. However, a few people continue to be responsive to God. Abram, one such person, is called by God from his homeland to a new country where he receives a number of amazing promises. While waiting for the fulfillment of God's promises, Abram experiences a number of exciting events, including a love triangle with Egypt's Pharaoh, a separation from his nephew to avoid a major conflict, a daring rescue mission, and some phenomenal conversations with the Lord.

Hand out copies of the reproducible sheet, "A Moving Experience." After kids complete the sheet, discuss the questions as a group. Try to help kids imagine the whirlwind of emotions that would go along with being forced to move suddenly. Deal first with their negative feelings, but then discuss new opportunities. What might they be able to do somewhere else that they would never be able to do if they stayed where they are? Try to have them empathize with Abram and his family—uprooted and probably confused, yet looking forward to unknown and exciting things in their new home.

DATE I USED THIS SESSION _____ GROUP I USED IT WITH _____

NOTES FOR NEXT TIME _____

_____

_____

Q&A

1. How many of you have ever moved? How did your former home(s) compare to where you are now? Get several responses. Also see if attitudes toward moving reflect the emotions connected to the reason for the move—a death, parents' divorce, loss of a job, etc.

2. If you'd been Abram when God called you away from your home (12:1-3), do you think you would have gone? Why or why not? (The promises sound good, but no destination is given. Some people might be suspicious or afraid.)

3. Based on Genesis 12:4-7, what do you think was the hardest part of the trip for Abram? (His age? Interaction with strange peoples? The size of his caravan?) What do you think was the best part? (The sense of adventure? The additional promise of God [the gift of the land] after arriving?)

4. You might think that Abram had so much faith that he would never be afraid of anything. Read Genesis 12:10-20 and explain why you think Abram allowed Sarai to be placed in such jeopardy. (Perhaps Abram's apparent fear for his own safety shows that he was certainly as human as anyone else.)

5. When the combined herds of Abram and his nephew, Lot, became too large to feed at the same spots, the two men decided to part company (13:1-12). What was significant about Abram's willingness to allow Lot to choose which way to go? (Lot's decision to settle in the better land placed him in the midst of other sinful settlers. Abram, on the other hand, was promised *all* of the land in the area.)

6. Lot's choice of homes soon caused problems when enemies carried him and his family away (14:1-12). But Abram came to the rescue (14:13-17). After Lot's rescue, Abram was confronted by two men (14:18-24). Why do you think he treated them so differently? (Melchizedek knew the true God, so Abram gave him a significant percentage of the spoils of battle. But Abram would have nothing to do with the wicked King of Sodom, lest his own good reputation become tarnished.)

7. How do you think Lot's capture and Abram's rescue affected the relationship between the two? (Perhaps Lot's choice of the better land had made him feel a bit selfish and guilty. If so, such feelings might only be intensified when he had to be rescued by Abram.)

8. Abram's continued faithfulness to God led to God's continued promises to him. At this point in their relationship, what promise did God add to His previous ones (15:1-5)? (The promise of a natural-born son—not an adopted one—and offspring that could not be counted.)

9. Genesis 15:6 is a significant verse that is quoted several times in the New Testament. What does it mean, and why is it so important? (Abram's faith was the single factor that allowed him to be placed in God's favor. The law would not be established until later. So Abram shows us that it's not following established rules that gets us into heaven, but by believing what God says.)

10. How did Abram know for sure that God meant what He promised (15:8-21)? (The smoking firepot [15:17] was an immediate sign. The eventual fulfillment of the prophecy [15:13, 14] was another.)

11. What are some things God has promised you? How do you know you can count on Him? What is the most difficult thing He expects from you?

Building faith is like building muscles—a person has to spend some time doing exercises until he or she gets stronger. Try to build some "spiritual muscles" in response to this story of Abraham. Have kids brainstorm some activities they can do as a group to serve God without expectation of an immediate reward. Rather than have a party that is scheduled, perhaps they can spend time serving food in a soup kitchen, putting together a program for a local nursing home, or gathering blankets for the homeless. God's commands to help others are clear as we read Scripture. Yet sometimes we need more faith (and perhaps a little push from a group leader) to actually *do* something.

A *MOVING*EXPERIENCE •••

You come home from school on what you think is a normal day, but you find your mother waiting for you. She explains that she's been offered a great new job and that your family is going to move. The trouble is, her company has offices all over the world—including Tibet, Morocco, Iceland, and New Zealand—and she doesn't know yet exactly where you'll be moving to. But the move will take place in three days, so that's all of the time you have to pack your stuff, tell everyone good-bye, and do everything else you need to do.

What do you think would be your immediate reaction to this news?

_____

_____

_____

What would be the three hardest things about the move?

_____

_____

_____

What things would you look forward to?

_____

_____

_____

What questions would you want answered before you move?

_____

_____

_____

Would you go willingly or reluctantly? Why?

_____

_____

_____

Would it make a difference if you knew your mom was going to get a huge salary (and triple your allowance), a luxurious company car that you could drive, and a brand new house that's four times the size of what you have now? Why?

_____

_____

_____

GENESIS 16

Womb for Rent

After receiving God's promise of a son, Abram seems to want to help make the promise come true. Since Sarai had not yet become pregnant, she suggests that he follow a custom of the times by impregnating her maidservant, Hagar. But Hagar's subsequent pregnancy causes tension between Sarai and Abram as well as between Sarai and Hagar. God intervenes to keep order in the house, yet the birth of Ishmael is only the beginning of conflict between Sarai and Hagar.

Call for three volunteers at a time—two girls and a guy. Have the girls both ask the guy out on a date, after which he must choose one of them. Each girl should explain where the date will be, what they will do, and why he should choose her over the other one. Before you begin, secretly explain to the guys that no matter what is said, they should choose the *shorter* of the two girls. After several trios have roleplayed the situation, ask: **How did it feel to be chosen over someone else? How did it feel to be rejected? How did it feel to have two people contending for your attention? How did it feel to discover that the only thing that mattered was height, and not any of the other things you mentioned?** Explain that in this session, a similar choice took place. But in this case, the main criterion was which woman could get pregnant.

DATE I USED THIS SESSION _____ GROUP I USED IT WITH _____

NOTES FOR NEXT TIME _____

_____

_____

1. Suppose God came to you in a dream and told you that when you are forty years old, you will become the president of the country. What do you think your life would be like between now and then? See whether your group members would plan to major in political science, run for Congress, or do other things to make the prophecy come true. Point out that when God says something will take place, He is capable of doing it with or without our "help."

2. What three words do you think you would use to describe your feelings if you were an old and childless woman in a time and place where women had no opportunities for fulfillment other than childbearing?

3. What can you tell about Sarai's feelings in verses 1 and 2? (She seems to blame God for her childlessness. She also seems to desperately want a family—both for herself and for Abram.)

4. Before you read any further in the chapter, can you predict what might happen when Abram sleeps with Hagar? Let group members who may not know the story speculate.

5. After Hagar became pregnant, why do you think she began to "despise" Sarai? (Perhaps she had mixed emotions, much like a surrogate mother today. The joy of becoming a mother would be weighed against giving up the baby to someone else.)

6. Since Sarai was the one who suggested the arrangement between Abram and Hagar, why do you think she blamed Abram (16:5)? (It's human nature for us to want to blame others for our own bad decisions.)

7. But Abram refused to take responsibility and left the problem for Sarai to handle. If you had been Sarai in this situation, what would you have done? What if you had been in Hagar's place? Compare answers to the actual responses of both women in verse 6.

8. We discover later that God's intention was for Abram *and Sarai* to have a child together. The child of Hagar is not the son who will inherit the promises God has given Abram. So why do you think God took care of them anyway (16:7-12)? (Hagar and Ishmael should not suffer because of someone else's bad decisions.)

9. The description of Ishmael (16:11, 12) may not sound like much, but it meant he was at least going to live. How do you think Hagar felt to know that they weren't going to completely miss out on God's blessings? What can we learn from her relationship with God? (We may tend to think that preachers and missionaries are God's "favorite" people, but each of us is just as important to Him.)

10. Names at this time were very important. Hagar, for example, called God "the God who sees me." And God named her son *Ishmael*, meaning "God hears." Based on your recent experiences with God, what would be a good name for Him? Based on your own behavior during this past week, what do you think He might name *you*?

11. Even though God worked out the immediate problem between Sarai and Hagar, their children continued to experience conflict. Ishmael's descendants became the Arabs, and Sarai's son's descendants became the Jews. What are some mistakes people make that can be forgiven, yet where the consequences continue to be a source of tension? (For example, a teenage girl can be forgiven for getting pregnant, yet the struggle she has raising the child would be ongoing.)

This is one of those stories in which no one comes off looking really good. The reproducible sheet, "Going for the Gold," challenges kids to decide which of the characters was most responsible for the problems they faced. (Kids should also consider their own behavior in each of the categories.) When they finish, let volunteers share in which categories they ranked themselves highest and lowest. Close with a prayer for wisdom—not only to solve the problems your group members already face, but also to avoid similar problems in the future.

G O I N G
for the
GOLD

Back when Abram lived, there weren't a lot of organized sports. The Olympics hadn't even been invented. But that didn't seem to keep people from competing in other activities. Below is a list of "events." In each event, three medals will be awarded: gold (first place), silver (second place), and bronze (third place). There are four people competing: Abram, Sarai, Hagar, and you. Give each event some serious thought. Based on what you've learned in this session and what you know about yourself, determine who gets which medals for each event.

EVENT	GOLD	SILVER	BRONZE
Getting into big trouble			
Dodging responsibility for one's own actions			
Trusting God when things don't seem to go right			
Enduring persecution from others			
Trying to avoid problems			
Coming up with great ideas that for some reason seem to go bad			
Showing humility			
Showing concern for others			
Showing forgiveness			
Complaining			

GENESIS 17

Couldn't We Just Sign a Contract?

After Abram has waited almost twenty-five years to become the "nation" that God had promised (12:2), the time nears for the birth of Isaac. Abram is now ninety-nine years old and a little doubtful. But God confirms His covenant with Abram by changing the names of both Abram and Sarai and by instituting the sign of circumcision.

(Needed: Temporary tattoos)

Provide group members with an assortment of "temporary tattoos" (available at most toy or novelty stores). Let each person choose one he or she feels is appropriate for his or her own unique personality. After applying the tattoos, let everyone model his or hers and explain why he or she chose it.
Ask: **In addition to the recent interest in personal tattoos, what other ways do people use to give clues to their interests and preferences?** (Makeup, clothing styles, T-shirts that promote favorite groups or hobbies, jewelry, etc.) Explain that this session will deal with another specific sign that differentiated one group of people from all others.

DATE I USED THIS SESSION _____ GROUP I USED IT WITH _____

NOTES FOR NEXT TIME _____

_____

_____

1. How many nicknames have you had in your life? How did you get them? Which ones did you dislike? Which ones were OK? Why do you think so many people have nicknames rather than using their given names?

2. Names were very important in Old Testament culture. Why do you think God changed the name of Abram ("exalted father") to Abraham ("father of many")? Why do you think God waited until Abraham was ninety-nine to change his name? (God's promise to Abram, made *twenty-four years ago*, was finally about to come true. The name change was one way to signify the event.)

3. God's part of the covenant was to give Abraham many descendants. What was Abraham supposed to do (17:1)? (Be obedient and blameless.) **Do you really think it's possible for someone to "be blameless"? Explain.** (Our goal is to have a reputation that's above blame.)

4. Have you ever been in a group or organization that required an initiation for membership? If so, what did you have to do to get in? What did Abraham have to do as a "sign of the covenant" (17:11) between himself and God? We tend to take circumcision for granted these days. But be honest—if you were a ninety-nine-year-old man and God told you to be circumcised to show your devotion to Him, what would you be thinking?

5. Why do you think God chose to use circumcision as a sign for His people? (The act of having the foreskin cut off would be symbolic of the people's separating themselves from other sinful nations and devoting themselves to God.)

6. Sarai's name was also changed at this time, though Sarai and Sarah both mean "princess." So why do you think God went to the trouble to rename her? (Isaac's birth would be a miracle. Her name change might be a reminder that not only was Abraham the father of nations, but that Sarah was the mother as well.)

7. When he heard that Sarah would get pregnant at age ninety, Abraham laughed at how ridiculous that sounded.

Are there stories or promises in the Bible that cause you to think, *Oh, don't be silly. That could never happen*? How do you deal with such portions of Scripture?

8. Abraham still showed a lot of concern for Ishmael, his son by Hagar (17:18-21). How do you think you would feel if you had one child singled out for greatness and another one who would do OK, but not nearly as well? How would you feel if you were the special child? How would you feel if you were the other one?

9. How long did it take Abraham to get himself and his household circumcised? (He got it done in one day.) **What can we learn from him about doing the things we *ought* to do, but may not exactly feel like doing?** (Some people may complain about finding time to have daily devotions, participate in service projects, and so forth. But anything God has commanded us to do should become a top priority.)

10. If you had been Abraham on this particular day when God spoke to him, what three words would you use to describe your feelings?

Abraham's circumcision was necessary if he was to be obedient. The reproducible sheet, "Picture This," asks kids to illustrate some of the things God expects from Christians. When everyone is finished, ask kids to display and explain their responses. Ask: **Which is worse—to do something God has said not to do, or not to do something God has said to do?** Obviously, both are equally bad. But sometimes we tend to focus more on the don'ts than the dos. We talk a lot about avoiding drinking, premarital sex, and such—which is fine, but we shouldn't stop there. If we want to stand out from the rest of the crowd (the purpose of circumcision), we need to move on to the dos—love our neighbors as ourselves, become the servant of all, turn the other cheek when offended, and so forth. Close by having kids brainstorm as many biblical commands as they can think of. Then ask God to help them become more faithful at fulfilling such commands. Only then will they begin to differentiate themselves from their peers and become identified as one of God's special people.

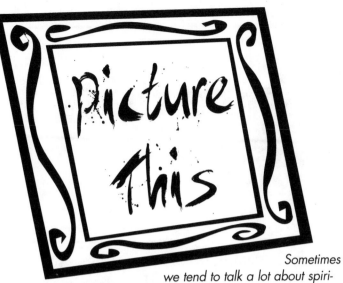

Sometimes we tend to talk a lot about spiritual things. Not this time. Using illustrations instead of words, see if you can answer the following questions. Your art work doesn't have to be great, but it should relate your feelings and/or experiences.

What is the *hardest* thing God could ask a person to do?

Circumcision was probably tough for Abraham. But so is cutting out past *sinful* activities when you become a Christian. What three things might a person find hardest to eliminate in order to serve God more faithfully?

What could a person do to indicate to *strangers* that he or she is a Christian?

What could a person do to indicate to his or her *friends* that he or she is a Christian?

If your faith in God was indicated by the size of your *muscles*, how would you look?

GENESIS 18–19

The Ultimate Urban Renovation

The sin of the cities of Sodom and Gomorrah becomes so blatant that God decides to destroy them. He shares His plan with Abraham, who immediately thinks of Lot and his family. Abraham negotiates with God to spare Sodom if certain conditions are met. Unfortunately, even those minimum conditions cannot be met. And even after God sends special messengers to rescue the few godly people remaining in Sodom, some of them are so distraught at leaving that they disobey God and suffer severe consequences.

Conduct a roleplay in which your kids represent members of a community that is promoting itself as "The Most Sinful City on Earth." Their goal is to draw as much tourism as possible by thinking of every possible sinful practice that people might want to participate in. First, kids should think of an appropriate name for their town. Then each person should come up with a "business" that would be likely to appeal to people looking to sin. If possible, kids should also create slogans for their businesses to make them sound as enticing as possible. Have some fun with this, but when you get to the part of the session describing the behavior of the men of Sodom, point out that the reality of sin is always abhorrent.

DATE I USED THIS SESSION _____ GROUP I USED IT WITH _____

NOTES FOR NEXT TIME _____

_____

_____

1. Have you ever had any bad or scary experiences while living in or visiting a large city? What do you think are the negative aspects of big cities? What are some of the positive aspects?

2. During Abraham's time, Sodom and Gomorrah were two of the most wicked cities in existence. Abraham was living outside these cities when he had three visitors. Who do you think they were (18:1-15)? (God is identified in verse 13. The other two were angels [19:1].)

3. First, God had a message for Sarah (18:9-15). What was it? How did she handle the news? (When she heard that she would have a baby, she laughed in disbelief, as Abraham had done previously [17:17].) Why was she so skeptical? (She was eighty-nine years old at the time [17:17].) Would you have been skeptical, or would you have believed God? Explain. (We like to think we have faith, yet most of us would be likely to doubt such news.)

4. Then God had a message for Abraham (18:16-21). Why do you think God shared His plans with Abraham? (Abraham's past faithfulness to God allowed God to trust him and treat him as a friend.)

5. How did Abraham take the news that God was about to judge Sodom and Gomorrah (18:22-33)? (He knew Lot and his family lived there, so Abraham negotiated with God to spare the city if ten righteous people could be found there.) How do your conversations with God differ from Abraham's?

6. When Lot confronted the two strangers—the angels—in Sodom, do you think his behavior seemed a bit suspicious (19:1-3)? Why? (His insistence that they not spend the night in the square indicates that he knew the dangers. Perhaps he also sensed that these were not ordinary men he was dealing with.)

7. Do you think homosexuality was simply an "alternative lifestyle" in Sodom (19:4-11)? (If anything, it seems to have been the *primary* lifestyle. The violence and group mentality described is frightening.)

8. What do you think about Lot? Was he still a good guy? (His strong stand against the crowd was commendable. But his offer to give up his virgin daughters was a terrible weakness, as was his willingness to remain in such a sinful place.)

9. God had sent two angels all the way to Sodom specifically to rescue Lot and his family. How did Lot's family show their gratitude (19:12-29)? (His prospective sons-in-law thought it was a joke. Lot, his wife, and two daughters literally had to be dragged out of the city. Lot argued about their destination. And his wife couldn't help but look back and suffer the consequences.)

10. You'd think that as Lot and his daughters looked at the smoking cities they'd be grateful and try to get off to a good new start. Why do you think that wasn't the case (19:30-38)? (Rather than becoming a positive example for others, Lot's family seems to have been affected by Sodom's sinful lifestyle.)

11. Describe a situation in which you were a positive example in the midst of wickedness. Describe a situation in which the negative influences of others rubbed off on you.

If we learn anything from Lot's story, it should be to listen and respond to God's warnings. The reproducible sheet, "Hard Changes," asks kids to evaluate how difficult it would be to give up a number of things. (Some are sinful activities; others are privileges.) Discuss the importance of changing our *attitudes* as well as our actions. While Lot's wife allowed herself to be removed from the sinful influences of Sodom, her heart remained there. When we make the changes God requests of us, we should never look back with regret.

HARDCHANGES

When God tells us to do something, we really ought to do it. Yet it seems that some people need more "incentive" than others. For example, Abraham voluntarily chose not to live in Sodom. Lot left, but only after a strong warning from God. Lot's wife and daughters had to be physically dragged away. And some people wouldn't leave under *any* conditions. Suppose you were asked to completely eliminate the following activities from your life. In each instance, how willing would you be to give up the activity if you sensed God wanted you to? (Check the appropriate column.)

What if you were asked to give this up?	No problem	I would want a clear warning from God	I would need to be forced by God	No way! I could never give this up
Gossiping				
Telling big, whopping lies				
Telling little white lies				
Putting down other people				
Challenging parental authority				
Watching TV				
Listening to music				
Eating sweets				

Involvement with sports				
Your favorite hobby				
Your education				
Your ability to drive				
Your boyfriend or girlfriend				
Drinking and smoking				
Thinking lustful thoughts				
Cheating on tests				
Copying homework				
Your money				

GENESIS 20; 26:1-11

Stand by Your Woman

The story of Abraham continues with an unflattering story very similar to a previous one (12:10-20). Once again, as Abraham fears for his life because of Sarah's beauty, he has her masquerade as his sister rather than his wife—even to the point of letting her be "picked up" by a king in the area. But God intervenes (again) and prevents Sarah from coming to physical harm or moral compromise. Then, to note an example of like-father-like-son behavior, we move forward in biblical history just far enough to see essentially the same story with Isaac and Rebekah.

Let volunteers take turns leading the group in a game of Simon Says. See who is best at causing the other group members to do things they don't actually want to do. Afterward, discuss the tendency most of us have to imitate other people—for good or for bad. (Use some specific examples of popular fashion or catchy words or phrases from the media.) Later, point out that we need to be careful not to adopt *undesirable* behavior. We need to learn to imitate the positive behavior of others without picking up bad habits.

DATE I USED THIS SESSION _____ GROUP I USED IT WITH _____

NOTES FOR NEXT TIME _____

_____

_____

Q&A

1. What are some mannerisms, sayings, facial expressions, or similar behaviors that you've picked up from your parents or other family members? Why do you suppose you started imitating those people—perhaps without even knowing it?

2. Abraham seems to have picked up a bad habit from somewhere. What was it (20:1, 2, 11-13)? (Telling foreign kings that his wife was really his sister out of fear of being killed by someone who wanted to take Sarah for his own.)

3. We know Abraham and Sarah had been married at least twenty-four years. Both had heard God say that Sarah would have Abraham's baby within the next year (18:10-12). Abraham had shown a lot of faith in God. So why do you think he would let some stranger walk away with his wife? (Fear is a powerful emotion. Sometimes we think we have our spiritual lives in order, but we don't seem to translate our faith to interpersonal, day-to-day events.)

4. Why do you think God held Abimelech responsible rather than Abraham (20:3)? (It hardly seems fair. However, Abimelech's actions would have been sinful whether or not he knew the truth.)

5. How did Abimelech discover the problem (20:4-7)? (God revealed the truth in a dream.) What would you have done at this point if you were King Abimelech? Would you do anything to Abraham and Sarah for their deception?

6. Abimelech seemed more concerned about the ethics of the situation than Abraham did (20:8-13). Do you think his "settlement" (20:14-16) was fair? What did he get in return (20:17, 18)?

7. You may have heard the sayings "History repeats itself" and "Like father, like son." Both are applicable years later as this story is repeated with Abraham's son, Isaac, and a different King Abimelech—probably the grandson of Abraham's peer. What are the similarities in Abraham's story and Isaac's? See Genesis 26:1-11. **What are the differences?** (Rebekah was never part of the "harem" as Sarah had been, though she was in danger of being pursued romantically by other men.)

8. **God had intervened directly for Sarah. This time He used a "coincidence." What prevented anyone from claiming Rebekah as a wife** (26:8, 9)**?** (Abimelech saw Isaac and Rebekah making out.)

9. **Since God wasn't so directly involved this time, what might you have done in Abimelech's place?** Compare group members' responses with Abimelech's actual response in Genesis 26:11. If no one mentions it, point out that again, a foreign king shows significant regard for morals and ethics.

10. **Who do you think felt worse in these situations: the men who allowed their wives to take great risks or the women who were in danger of bigamy or worse? Explain.**

11. **Would you, under any conditions, permit someone you loved to be threatened? Why or why not? What would it take for you to allow such a risk?**

Fear is a deceptive emotion. It's usually something we try to hide; yet it is so powerful that if we don't suffer from fear itself, we frequently suffer from trying to avoid fear. And what we don't realize is that *others* may suffer because of *our* fears. Sarah and Rebekah certainly found that out. The reproducible sheet, "Some of All Fears," challenges group members to see for themselves what fear can cause people to do. When they finish, let them share responses. Then challenge them to think of their own strongest fears and how they (and other people) might be more affected by those fears than they realize. If some of them are willing, let volunteers confess their fears and any potential consequences they can think of.

SOME OF ALL Fears

1. Cindy has a severe **fear of spiders.** She won't go in the basement or attic of her house. If anything brushes against her arm that remotely feels like a spider web, she shrieks in **horror** and disgust. She doesn't know where the fear came from. It's just there. But just today she was invited by her best friends to go on a youth group retreat with their church. It's out in the woods among some of the prettiest scenery in the state. Cindy loves her friends. She loves the woods and lakes and rivers. But she knows there are spiders in those woods. She quickly told her friends no—so quickly, in fact, that they looked quite hurt by her instant rejection of their proposal. Do you think Cindy's feelings and actions are justified? If she confided her fear to you, what advice would you give her? How does her fear of spiders affect *other* people?

2. Joe is afraid that other **people won't like him.** He goes out of his way to do things for other people, including buying them stuff and doing favors to encourage them to hang around. He doesn't really have to work so hard because he's naturally likable. But lately he's started doing risky and potentially **dangerous** things to get attention— jumping from high places, riding on the hoods of friends' cars, and stuff like that. He tries not to be *too* stupid about what he does; it's just that his fear drives him to try too hard. The problem is that Joe has two younger brothers who look up to him and want to be just like him. They've noticed his strange behavior lately, but haven't yet begun to imitate him. If Joe were your close friend, what would you tell him? How could he deal with his fear? How does his fear of not being liked affect *other* people?

3. Ramona is afraid her parents are **going to get divorced.** She's their only child, and feels she must be partly to blame. So now she's spending almost all her spare time with one parent or the other. Her **grades have dropped** significantly, she has dropped out of cheerleading, and she hardly ever goes out with her friends anymore. But she can't tell that she's doing any good, and her fear is as strong as ever. What would you tell her to try to help her feel better? How does her fear of her parents' possible divorce affect *other* people?

4. Think of one of your current fears. What are some ways you can think of that your fear might affect other people?

GENESIS 21–22

You Win Son, You (Almost) Lose Son

Abraham and Sarah finally receive the son they have been promised. Isaac's birth increases the tension between Sarah and Hagar, resulting in the departure of Hagar and Ishmael. God commands Abraham to sacrifice young Isaac to Him. Abraham dutifully obeys, but at the last possible moment, God stops Abraham from slaying the boy.

(Needed: Prize)

Have some kind of contest in which kids compete to win a better-than-average prize. After a while, announce the winner and hand him or her the prize. But then you should "discover" that you have time for another round. Compete a while longer and announce the winner again—preferably, a different person. Hand that person the prize. But then "double check" the scores and announce that you had miscalculated, allowing the prize to go to yet another person. When kids complain, pretend to be frustrated and take the prize back, explaining that no one gets it. After a moment, confess that the game was a "setup." Return the prize to the first person who won it and continue with the session. Explain that God gave Isaac to Abraham, and then it seemed that He would take him back.

DATE I USED THIS SESSION _____ GROUP I USED IT WITH _____

NOTES FOR NEXT TIME _____

_____

_____

1. What kinds of things do you really look forward to? Have you ever really looked forward to something, only to have it ruined for you when the day or event finally arrived? If so, what happened? How did you feel?

2. Sarah was ninety years old and had wanted to be a mother all of her life. Abraham had been promised by God twenty-five years ago that he would become "a great nation" (12:2). How do you think they felt when Isaac was finally born (21:1-7)?

3. If reporters were covering this story today, what do you suppose would be the headline of their report?

4. Not *everyone* was happy when Isaac was born. When you think about the other members of Abraham's household, what problems might you expect (21:8-10)? If no one mentions it, point out that Ishmael was thirteen at this time—not a good age to deal with rejection.

5. God took care of Hagar and Ishmael. How and why did He do it (21:11-21)? (Ishmael was the offspring of Abraham, so God promised to give him many descendants—even though he wouldn't be the one through whom God would fulfill His covenant with Abraham.)

6. Sarah's wish had come true. But how do you think Abraham felt as he lost the son he had raised for the past thirteen years?

7. Perhaps Abraham was consoled somewhat about Ishmael's loss with the birth of Isaac. But what happened several years later that might have caused Abraham to be concerned again (22:1, 2)? (He was instructed by God to sacrifice Isaac as a burnt offering.)

8. Do you think Abraham may have questioned God's instructions or perhaps argued a bit? (We know that Abraham was quick to obey God's command, because he started out "early the next morning" [22:3]. But we don't know what his state of mind was. Perhaps he got started early because he was up all night worrying!)

49

9. Why was Isaac called Abraham's "only son" (22:2, 12, 16)? (Isaac was the only son of Abraham and Sarah—the one intended to inherit the things God had promised Abraham.)

10. Why in the world would a father be willing to kill his son just because God said to? Point out that Hebrews 11:17-19 tells us that Abraham so strongly trusted God to fulfill His promise that he knew God would raise Isaac from the dead, if necessary.

11. Read Genesis 22:3-10. Only one comment from Isaac is given. But put yourself in his place and describe what you think he was feeling as he and Abraham walked up the mountain . . . as Abraham began to tie him up . . . as he lay on the altar looking around . . . and as his own father raised a knife to kill him. Try to create the appropriate emotions for such an experience, but don't provide any "easy answers" at this point. Kids should struggle with this a bit as they complete the reproducible sheet that follows.

Hand out copies of the reproducible sheet, "Child Endangerment." Let kids consider whether or not the story of Abraham's willingness to offer Isaac could take place today. Afterward, ask: Why would God *ever* ask someone to do what He asked of Abraham? Wasn't that a horrific form of child abuse? Doesn't the request go against everything we know about God's nature? Kids should see that Abraham was very special to God. God and Abraham had spent twenty-five years building a relationship and establishing a one-of-a-kind covenant. Perhaps God's instructions to Abraham were a way of allowing one special person to get a glimpse of how God feels. God had already destroyed the earth with a flood and had rained burning sulfur on Sodom and Gomorrah. And eventually, to provide a more lasting solution for the sinfulness of humans, God would sacrifice *His* one and only Son, whom He loved. He shared with Abraham what that would feel like—both the pain and the joy that were involved. Close in prayer, thanking God for His willingness to provide a perfect and lasting sacrifice, even though it surely caused Him great distress to do so.

ENDAN*child*ERMENT

Your best friend comes up to you with a rather strange look in his or her eyes. "I've come to say good-bye," he or she says. You are shocked, and wait to hear about a parent's job opportunity or some other emergency that would necessitate having the person move away. But that's not the case.

Your friend says, "You know how my family and I started going to that new church that meets out in the woods? Well, they have this practice where, once every ten years or so, one very, very faithful family is chosen to sacrifice one of its children to God. I can't believe it, but my family was chosen! I'm going to be sacrificed this weekend. I'm not supposed to say anything to anyone, but I just wanted you to know why I'm not going to be around any more. You've got to promise to keep this a secret!"

Your friend has that look in his or her eye that always comes when his or her mind is made up. But you know you've got to do something.

What would you say to your friend (as soon as you were able to speak)?

_____
_____
_____
_____

What questions would you want him or her to think through?

_____
_____
_____
_____

If there seemed to be no way to change your friend's mind, what would you do then? Would you keep the secret? Would you go to authorities?

_____
_____
_____
_____

Suppose your friend uses the story of Abraham and Isaac as a defense. ("If God doesn't want us to go through with this, He will stop us.") What would you say to that? Is there a difference between faith back then and faith today?

_____
_____
_____

GENESIS 24

The Old "Water Your Camels" Pick-up Line

Sarah has died. Abraham is getting older and realizes it's time to prepare Isaac to inherit God's blessings on their family. Not wanting his son to get a wife from the surrounding idolatrous nations, Abraham arranges to find Isaac a young woman from his homeland. Abraham's servant then witnesses God at work in a clear and powerful way—even in the "mundane" matter of romance and young love.

Distribute copies of the reproducible sheet, "Blind Date." Give group members a few minutes to fill it out. Then ask volunteers to share their responses. Lead in to a discussion on whether blind dates are good or bad. Ask your group members to share some experiences they (or people they know) have had with blind dates. (You might want to be ready with a few stories of your own.)

DATE I USED THIS SESSION _____ GROUP I USED IT WITH _____

NOTES FOR NEXT TIME _____

_____

_____

1. Would you ever allow one or both of your parents to set you up on a blind date? Why or why not? Would you ever, under any circumstances, consider an arranged marriage in which one or both of your parents set you up with someone you've never seen? Why or why not?

2. If your parents *were* to pick someone out for you, what criteria do you think they would use? Imagine the person they might choose and describe his or her physical characteristics, interests, and other qualities. Compare group members' responses with Abraham's criteria (24:1-9).

3. What if you were given the assignment to pick out a spouse for your best friend? Where would you go to find this spouse? How would you describe your best friend to the person you picked out? What would you say to the person to convince him or her to marry your best friend? Compare group members' responses to Abraham's servant's prayerful concern for finding just the right person (24:10-14).

4. How long did it take for God to provide a likely candidate to be Isaac's wife (24:15)? (Abraham's servant wasn't even finished *asking* before Rebekah showed up.) **What were Rebekah's qualifications (24:15, 16)?** (She was beautiful, a virgin, a good worker, and came from a good family. [She was Abraham's grandniece.])

5. Hospitality was a good characteristic for a prospective wife. To offer a stranger a drink of water was admirable. But Abraham's servant had *ten* thirsty camels (24:10). The water had to be drawn by hand from a well and carried to a trough (24:20). Do you think Rebekah expected anything for her hospitality? How do you suppose she felt when this stranger started handing her gold jewelry and asking to spend the night (24:22, 23)? What would you have done in her place?

6. Dealing with an innocent young girl is one thing. Now Abraham's servant had to deal with her male protectors—specifically her brother (24:24-33). Do you think he felt any nervousness about meeting the rest of her family? Why or why not?

7. Abraham's servant wouldn't even eat until he could tell the *whole* story to the rest of the family (24:32-49). When he *finally* finished, Rebekah's brother and father made a deal with him (24:50-54). If you had been in Rebekah's place at that point, what would you have done?

8. How do we know that Rebekah even *wanted* to leave home to marry some man she had never seen before (24:55-58)? (Abraham's servant wanted to return right away. Rebekah's family wanted her to hang around for a couple more weeks. When they left the final decision up to her, she was ready to ride.)

9. Rebekah wasn't completely alone. She had a nurse and more than one attendant. But it still must have been a strange experience. What do you suppose she thought about on the long ride to meet Isaac?

10. Isaac and Rebekah were married right away. And even though they didn't always see eye-to-eye, the marriage lasted. If, by some weird set of circumstances, you ever agreed to an arranged marriage with someone you've never seen before, what do you think it would take to make it work? How many camels or other units of exchange or possessions do you think you would be worth?

Ask: **Do you think God still brings people together today like He did for Isaac and Rebekah? Do you believe there's one specific person of the opposite sex somewhere waiting to find or be found by you? If so, how eager are you to meet him or her? If not, how can you know what kind of person is right for you? If you believe that God wants you to remain single, how might the principles in this Bible story apply to your friendships?** Help your kids see that God is deeply concerned about their romantic feelings and relationships. After all, He is the only one who fully understands love. Challenge your kids to do whatever it takes to please God in their dating lives and receive His blessing on their activities and relationships.

If you were going to set up your best friend on a blind date, what kind of person would you look for? Fill out the following information.

On a scale of 1 to 10 (1 = "Yuk"; 10 = "Whoa"), how good-looking would the person be? _____

On a scale of 1 to 10 (1 = Homer Simpson; 10 = Albert Einstein), how intelligent would the person be? _____

On a scale of 1 to 10 (1 = library dweller; 10 = party animal), how "wild" would the person be? _____

This person's personality would be a cross between _____ and _____.
(For instance, someone who is caring and also has a sense of humor might be a cross between Mother Teresa and Robin Williams.)

This person's looks would be a cross between _____ and _____.

This person's body would be a cross between _____ and _____.

This person's style of dress would be a cross between _____ and _____.

This person would be able to carry on an intelligent conversation about
_____.

This person *must* _____
_____.

This person *must not* _____
_____.

GENESIS 25:19–28:9

Family Feud

In the beginning of Genesis 25, Abraham leaves everything he owns to Isaac, while token gifts were given to the other sons. Now, as the Bible moves to the next generation, we are whisked directly to the passing of Isaac's blessing to one very unlikely recipient—Jacob. Being the second-born son, Jacob wouldn't ordinarily be the rightful heir. But he receives Isaac's blessing anyway as he tricks his older brother Esau out of his birthright and blessing. Esau retaliates with a plot to take Jacob's life, forcing Jacob to leave his family and home.

Hand out the reproducible sheet, "Them's Feudin' Words!" to group members as they arrive. Give them a few minutes to fill in their responses. When everyone is finished, ask for volunteers to *roleplay* the situations (two volunteers per situation). Give your actors a few minutes to think through how they would feel, what they would say, and how they would react in their assigned situation. After all of the volunteers have performed, say: **Family problems can be pretty difficult to resolve. Two of the Bible characters we'll be looking at today, Jacob and Esau, knew this firsthand.** Rather than reading the entire passage, you may want to summarize the story for your group members and focus specifically on the Scripture passages mentioned in the "Q & A" section.

DATE I USED THIS SESSION _____ GROUP I USED IT WITH _____

NOTES FOR NEXT TIME _____

_____

_____

1. What is unusual about God's statement that the older brother would serve the younger (25:23)? (In Jacob's day, the oldest son received special privileges and rights. In a sense, younger sons "served" the firstborn. God's choosing Jacob shows that He is not bound by human tradition.)

2. What does the "stew incident" tell you about Jacob? (He was a schemer, always thinking about how he could gain an advantage over others.) **What does it tell you about Esau?** (He cared very little about his birthright.)

3. According to Genesis 26:34, 35, how did Isaac and Rebekah feel about Esau's wives? (Esau's wives were a "source of grief" to his parents.) **What kinds of things today can be a source of grief to parents?** (Alcohol and drug use, hanging around with the wrong crowd, getting involved in the occult, dating the wrong type of people, etc.)

4. In Genesis 25:23, God told Rebekah that Esau would one day serve Jacob. Do you think Jacob's trickery and deception were part of God's plan? Why or why not? (God didn't need Jacob's "help" in accomplishing His plan. Besides, nowhere does the passage indicate that Jacob was working for anything other than his own personal gain.)

5. God worked out His plan for Jacob's life despite Jacob's scheming nature and other imperfections. What are some imperfections in your life that God has to work around to get His will done?

6. Why do you suppose Rebekah helped Jacob in his deception of Isaac? (Perhaps because Jacob was her favorite. [See Genesis 25:28.]) **What are some modern-day examples of parents showing favoritism to certain kids? What kinds of problems does favoritism cause in families?**

7. When Isaac asked Jacob—thinking it was Esau—how he found the game so quickly, how did Jacob reply? ("The Lord your God gave me success" [27:20].) **Do you think there's any significance to the fact that Jacob used the phrase "The Lord *your* God"? Explain.** (Perhaps Jacob didn't recognize God personally at this point in his life.)

8. What is the significance of Isaac's blessing in Genesis 27:29: "Be lord over your brothers"? (By blessing Jacob, Isaac is unwittingly fulfilling God's promise to Rebekah in Genesis 25:23.)

9. The tradition of this time was that having a birthright inevitably led to receiving a father's blessing. Esau had already sold Jacob his birthright for some food (25:29-34), so why do you think Esau was so upset to learn that Jacob had gotten the blessing? (Perhaps he was angry at having been deceived.)

10. When Isaac realized that Jacob had deceived him (27:30-35), why didn't Isaac just take back the blessing? (The spoken word of blessing or curse was seen as a very powerful reality. It wasn't a contract that could be undone. Once it was spoken, it became reality.)

11. Even though Jacob was blessed, he still had to deal with the trouble he had with Esau (27:41-45). How do you feel about the idea that God's blessing doesn't take away life's troubles? (Anxious about the future, confident of God's protection, etc.)

(Needed: Index cards)

Distribute index cards and pencils. Ask each group member to write down a conflict (or potential conflict) that is currently brewing between him or her and one of his or her family members. It may be a disagreement about what time curfew should be, a parent's objection to the person his or her child is dating, or something else. Then have each person consider what the possible consequences might be if the conflict isn't resolved. For an extreme example of what can become of unresolved conflict, refer group members back to Genesis 27:41. Ask for volunteers to share what they wrote; however, don't force anyone to respond. Then encourage your group members to pray about their conflicts (or potential conflicts), asking God for wisdom and strength in resolving them.

Them's FEUDIN' Words!

Family life can be hard—even for Christians. Read the following situations and describe what you would do if you were one of the people involved.

FAMILY FEUD #1

Characters: Vanessa and her mom
Situation: Vanessa arrived home at 2 A.M.—four hours past her curfew! She claims there is a good reason for her being late. Her mom is ready to discipline Vanessa by taking away all privileges—including the phone.

If I were Vanessa, I would . . .

If I were Vanessa's mom, I would . . .

FAMILY FEUD #2

Characters: Raoul and his dad
Situation: Raoul is really involved in the youth group and hasn't been spending much time at home. His dad is upset that Raoul isn't completing his responsibilities around the house. Raoul feels his dad should support his interest in the church.

Raoul's dad wants the chores done on time.

If I were Raoul, I would . . .

If I were Raoul's dad, I would . . .

FAMILY FEUD #3

Characters: Dave and Lisa (brother and sister)
Situation: Dave finds Lisa's diary and reads his sister's confession of some pretty serious sin. Lisa has confessed the sin to God and has been forgiven. But Dave is threatening to tell their parents about what he discovered.

If I were Dave, I would . . .

If I were Lisa, I would . . .

GENESIS 28:10-22

Promises, Promises

Genesis 28 begins with Isaac calling Jacob in to bless him and send him on a journey for a wife. The end of chapter 27 reminds us of the human conflict motivating this journey— fear of Esau. Jacob receives Isaac's blessing. Ironically, the blessing includes possession of the land—the same land that Jacob is being sent away from. While on his journey, Jacob has a dream. In the dream, God makes a promise to Jacob. This promise goes beyond the blessing of Abraham, the blessing of land and offspring. Because of the conflict Jacob is facing, God also promises His presence and protection to Jacob.

Give copies of the reproducible sheet, "The People's Court: The Case of the Bogus Blessing" to four of your group members. Assign parts and, if possible, give your actors a few minutes to read through the skit and prepare. When they're ready, have them perform. Afterward, say: **Sometimes it may seem like God has abandoned us. We may even feel like filing a suit against God for breach of contract. However, God promises to protect us in our darkest hours. He did for Jacob. Let's take a closer look at this story.** Have your group read Genesis 28:10-22.

DATE I USED THIS SESSION _____ GROUP I USED IT WITH _____

NOTES FOR NEXT TIME _____

_____

_____

1. Put yourself in Jacob's position. You've just received the blessing from your father that God promised to you when you were born. Unfortunately, you don't have time to celebrate because you're too busy running for your life from your brother. How would you feel? Why?

2. God chose to talk to Jacob in a dream (28:12). Why do you suppose He chose a dream as His method of communication? (While Jacob was asleep, he was a "captive" listener. God had Jacob's full attention.) **Do you think God still communicates to people through dreams? Why or why not? Have you ever felt that God communicated to you through a dream? Explain.**

3. Genesis 28:12 describes the original "Stairway to Heaven." How do you think Jacob felt seeing not only the angels ascending and descending, but God Himself? (It's likely that at this point in his life, Jacob didn't recognize the Lord as *his* God, so he may have been a little frightened by God's sudden appearance.)

4. God first reminds Jacob of His relationship to Abraham and Isaac (28:13). The Lord had been faithful to them and He would be faithful to Jacob. What are some ways God has helped you in the past? How do those past experiences help you when you face troubles today?

5. Unlike the blessings given to Abraham and Isaac, Jacob's blessing included God's protection. Why do you think God included this feature in Jacob's blessing? (Because of Jacob's situation, he *needed* protection; Abraham and Isaac might have had less need of it.) **What does this tell you about the blessings of God?** (They are "customized." He gives us exactly what we need when we need it.)

6. If God were going to give you a blessing for your current situation, what might that blessing include? (Strength to deal with parents' divorce? Concentration to be able to study for an important test? Courage to be a witness around non-Christian friends?)

7. What motivated Jacob to worship God (28:16-19)? (Fear.) **Do you think fear should be a motivator for us to worship God? Why or why not? What motivates *you* to worship God?**

8. What do you notice about Jacob's vow to God (28:20-22)? (It seems very conditional—*if* you do this for me, then I will do something for You.) **What kinds of conditions do people today place on their obedience to God?** (*If* something's popular with other people; *if* it's convenient; *if* it's safe; *if* it's easy; etc.)

9. In Matthew 4:6, 7, Satan tempts Jesus to throw Himself off the highest point of the temple, reasoning that God would send angels to catch Him. Jesus replies by referring to Deuteronomy 6:16: "Do not put the Lord your God to the test." With this in mind, would you say that Jacob is putting God "to the test" with his conditional vow (28:20-22)? Explain.

10. What does Jacob offer God in return for God's protection and provision (28:22)? (He offers to give back a tenth of all that God gives him.) **What is the significance of Jacob's vow?** (Giving back a tenth of his possessions is a way of acknowledging God as his Lord.) **What kinds of things keep people today from tithing—giving back a tenth of what God has provided for them?** (Selfishness, concern about not having enough money to pay for the things we "need," not understanding the importance of generous giving, unwillingness to give money to the church, etc.)

Say: **We've all had—and will continue to have—hard times in our lives. These are the times in which we need to trust God to intervene.** Ask kids to call out some situations in which a person might have a hard time trusting God. After kids have listed several situations, go through the list as a group, brainstorming ways God might intervene in each situation. Close the session in prayer, asking God to help us remember His promises to us and to help us trust in Him during times of difficulty.

The People's Court:
The Case of the Bogus Blessing

DOUG (to audience): Hello, I'm Doug Lewmellon and this is *The People's Court*. Welcome to "The Case of the Bogus Blessing." Entering our courtroom today is the plaintiff, Jake. *[Jake enters.]* Jake complains that after receiving God's blessing, which promised children and land, the blessing malfunctioned and turned into a curse. Rather than receiving land and children, Jake was instead threatened by his brother Esau and actually had to flee the land promised him. The defendant is God. *[God enters.]* God says that Jake doesn't understand God's ways. God's defense is simple: Jake can't get what God has promised until God sees fit to give it.

JUDGE (to Jake): I've read your complaint, sir. You say the defendant promised a blessing to you and failed to deliver a working model?

JAKE: That's putting it lightly. One minute dear old Dad, rest his soul, is saying how much land I get, and the next minute I'm running out of town for fear of my life! Not only didn't I get the land, but I also lost my family and my security! I'll probably have to use a rock for a pillow tonight! And do you know how cold it gets here at night?

JUDGE: Wait a minute! Your suit is against God. If your dad is the one who blessed you, why aren't you suing him?

JAKE: The blessing my dad gave me was passed on to him by Grandpa Abraham, who got the blessing from God. It just keeps getting passed down. If I'm blessed, then let me be blessed. But I don't see how having my brother put a price on my head is being blessed!

JUDGE (to God): Is that correct? Did You pronounce a blessing on the plaintiff's grandfather?

GOD: Not only did I pronounce it on Abraham and Isaac, but I am also ready to promise my faithfulness to Jake. Unfortunately, he's so self-centered that I haven't been able to get a word in edgewise. I'll probably have to wait until he's asleep if I want to say anything. *(To Himself)* Hey, that's not a bad idea. I'll talk to him when he can't talk back!

JUDGE (to God): Is it true that once Jake was blessed,

You allowed him to be hunted by his brother and forced to leave the land You promised him?

GOD: Sure. That's the problem with Jake. He can't wait for anything. But He'll get patience before you know it, though. I promised him land and family, and I'll deliver. But it will happen the way *I* want it to happen.

JUDGE (to Jake): Anything you'd like to add?

JAKE: Listen, Judge. I hear what He's saying. But that doesn't change the fact that I have nowhere to sleep tonight! I think He ought to pay up right now.

JUDGE: We'll take a short break, and I'll be back to give you my decision. *[Judge exits.]*

DOUG (to audience): Well, what do you think? Should Jake get his just deserts or spend the night in the desert? We'll find out in a moment!
[Judge Whopper enters and sits down.]

JUDGE (to Jake): I understand your concern, Jake. It doesn't seem like God is following through on His promise. But I looked it up in the Book, and God's right. What He promises, He does. You just have to trust Him as He completes His plan. Sleep on it. Maybe you'll get a revelation or something. My suggestion is to lay your head on a nice, comfortable rock and see what happens. My judgment is for the defendant.

DOUG (to audience): Well, there you have it. God is trusted to keep His promises. Jake will have to trust God to bless Him even when it seems like the blessing is bogus. For *The People's Court*, I'm Doug Lewmellon.

GENESIS 29–31

Now That's Commitment!

OVERVIEW

After fleeing his homeland, Jacob falls in love with Rachel, Laban's daughter. Jacob works for Laban for seven years in order to marry her. But Jacob is tricked and ends up marrying Leah, Laban's older daughter, instead. Jacob works another seven years in order to marry Rachel. After Rachel gives birth to Joseph, Jacob decides to return to his homeland.

OPENING ACT

(Needed: Two boxes of chocolate)

Hold an auction. Display two boxes of chocolate (one of which is nearly empty) that will go to the highest bidders. Kids will "bid" by offering to do stunts. The more outrageous the stunt, the higher the "bid." Auction off the nearly empty box first. After the highest bidder has performed his or her stunt, award him or her the box of chocolates. (Be prepared for some complaining.) Before you auction off the second box, show kids that it's full. Then auction it off. Afterward, explain that Jacob faced a similar situation. He worked seven years for Laban in order to marry Rachel. But when he finally got what he'd been working for, he found out it wasn't what he wanted—it was Leah, Rachel's older sister. So Jacob had to work another seven years in order to marry Rachel.

DATE I USED THIS SESSION _____ GROUP I USED IT WITH _____

NOTES FOR NEXT TIME _____

_____

_____

Q&A

1. Have you ever bought or ordered something, only to find out later that it wasn't what you wanted? If so, what happened? What did you do about it?

2. Do you think working seven years was a fair "price" for Jacob to pay in order to marry Rachel (29:18-20)? Why or why not? Would *you* work for seven years to earn the right to marry someone? Why or why not?

3. What clue do we get in Genesis 29:21 that Jacob was saving himself sexually for Rachel? (His words, "My time is completed, and I want to lie with her," indicate that after seven years, he was ready to consummate the relationship.)

4. How do you think Jacob was able to wait so long for sex? (Perhaps his love was deeper than mere physical attraction. Perhaps he was committed to God's plan for the future.) Do you think it's easier or harder to postpone sex until after marriage in today's society? Explain.

5. How could Jacob have not realized that he was with Leah, and not Rachel (29:23)? (It was dark when he "lay" with her. Perhaps Leah was wearing a veil.)

6. How do you think Jacob felt the next morning when he found Leah lying next to him? (Angry at Laban; disappointed; foolish for allowing himself to be deceived.) What would you have done if you were Jacob? Why?

7. How would you describe Laban? Why? (Laban was sneaky, deceitful, and concerned only with his own interests. In other words, he was a lot like Jacob.) Why do you suppose God allowed Laban to take advantage of Jacob? (Perhaps to teach Jacob a lesson about deception. After all, Jacob had deceived his own father and brother.)

8. After Jacob married Rachel, Leah was kind of pushed to the background. How do you think she felt? (Unloved, perhaps a bit desperate to earn Jacob's love.) How did God bless Leah (29:31-35)? (He opened her womb and allowed her to have children.) Do you think this made Leah feel better? Why or why not?

9. Rachel was so afraid of not having children that she took matters into her own hands. What did she do? (She gave Jacob her maidservant, Bilhah, to sleep with. Also, the mandrake plant that Reuben found was thought to magically induce preganancy. That's why Rachel was so desperate to eat it.) Why do you think people have a hard time waiting for God to answer their prayers? (They would rather follow their own timetable, rather than God's. When people can't physically see or hear God, they may assume that He can't see or hear them.)

11. Genesis 30:22 says that "God remembered Rachel." Have you ever felt as if God has forgotten about you? If so, what did you do? In Genesis 30:25, after the birth of Joseph, the family of Jacob was almost complete. Rachel later gave birth to one other son, Benjamin (35:18). Let's take a moment now to sort out the confusing relationships of Jacob's offspring. Hand out copies of the reproducible sheet, "Family Tree." Give kids a few minutes to work on it. When everyone is finished, go through the answers. (Leah— [1] Reuben, [2] Simeon, [3] Levi, [4] Judah, [9] Issachar, [10] Zebulun, [11] Dinah; Bilhah—[5] Dan, [6] Naphtali; Zilpah—[7] Gad, [8] Asher; Rachel—[12] Joseph, [13] Benjamin. Judah was the direct ancestor of David and Jesus.)

13. Jacob gave God the credit for his prosperity and protection from Laban (31:42). Why are people tempted to take the credit for their successes instead of giving God the credit? (Some refuse to see God's work in their lives. Others are too proud to admit that they were helped by God.)

Say: **After having been protected and provided for by God, Jacob finally acknowledges that the Lord is *his* God.** Distribute paper and pencils. Ask kids who are Christians to write down what it took before they recognized the Lord personally. Ask those who aren't Christians to write down what it would take before they will recognize the Lord personally. After a few minutes, collect the sheets. Read a few of the responses aloud—without identifying the author. Close in prayer, thanking God for making Himself known in our lives.

family TREE

Arranging Jacob's wives, children, and maidservants for a family portrait will take some work. Try to help as much as possible by matching each of Jacob's children with the woman who gave birth to him or her. For extra credit, number the kids from 1 to 12 according to the order in which they were born. For extra-extra credit, circle the son who was the direct ancestor of David and Jesus.

GENESIS 32

Anticipation

Only one person stands in the way of Jacob's return to his homeland—Esau, his brother. After being reassured by angels of God's protection, Jacob sends messengers ahead to tell Esau that he's coming home. When Esau begins to come toward Jacob with four hundred men, Jacob reminds God of His promise to protect him. The night before his meeting with Esau, stubborn Jacob "wrestles" with God, and receives from God both a blessing and a minor hip injury.

(Needed: Magazines, poster board, scissors, tape)

Have kids form teams. Give each team several magazines, a piece of poster board, scissors, and tape. Say: **We all have things that scare us or make us anxious. You have three minutes to find as many things in these magazines that might "scare" you or make you worried. Cut out as many of these as you can and attach them to your poster board. At the end of three minutes, the team with the most scary things wins.** Afterward, have each team display and explain its pictures. Then say: **Sometimes our anticipation causes us to question whether or not God is taking care of us. Jacob experienced this as he prepared to meet Esau—the brother he tricked out of his blessing and birthright.**

DATE I USED THIS SESSION _____ GROUP I USED IT WITH _____

NOTES FOR NEXT TIME _____

_____

_____

1. Have you ever had a big fight or a "falling out" with a friend or family member? If so, what was it like the next time you saw that person? What if *twenty years* had gone by between the time of your falling out and the next time you saw the person? What might your reunion be like?

2. If you were Jacob, how do you think you would have felt coming face to face with the angels (32:1, 2)? (The experience may have been unsettling for Jacob, but he'd already had at least one encounter with angels before [28:10-15].)

3. The angels' appearance made Jacob feel pretty confident that God was with Him (32:1, 2). Have you ever had times when you were convinced that God was right there with you? If so, what was it like?

4. What do you think Jacob was expecting Esau to do upon hearing the news of Jacob's return (32:1-5)?

5. In Jacob's prayer (32:9-12), he reminds God of His promise of protection. Do you think Jacob was praying for his own benefit or for God's? (Perhaps he was reassuring himself when he reminded God of His promise. Or perhaps he was demonstrating his trust in God and admitting that he needed God's intervention.) **When you are in trouble, what promises of God do you stand on?**

6. Even though Jacob prayed for God's intervention, he wasn't taking any chances. He sent some peace offerings ahead for Esau (32:13-21). **How do you think God felt about Jacob's action?** (Perhaps He didn't mind Jacob's attempt to win his brother's affection. Or perhaps He was disappointed in Jacob's lack of trust in Him.)

7. In verses 22-25, we read that Jacob got into a wrestling match with a man who turned out to be God. Scripture says that the man could not overpower Jacob. But surely God could have beaten Jacob, right? **What do you think this passage is saying?** (Jacob was stubborn. He was not about to give up.) **Why do you think God hurt Jacob's hip?** (It was a reminder to Jacob that he was wrestling someone who was much more powerful than he.)

8. Jacob boldly asks this "man" to bless him (32:26-29). Are you this bold when it comes to asking God to bless you? Why or why not?

9. The name *Israel* means "he struggles with God." God gave Jacob a name that reflected the kind of relationship he had with God. If God were to rename you according to the kind of relationship you have with Him, what name would He give you?

10. How do you think Jacob felt when he realized he had actually been wrestling with God? How would you have felt? (Frightened? Excited? In awe of seeing God face to face? Puzzled?)

Distribute copies of the reproducible sheet, "Wrestle Mania!" Instruct group members to choose an area of their life that they are "wrestling" with right now. Then instruct them to come up with a strategy, based on the accompanying Scripture passages, for wrestling with this area. After a few minutes, have volunteers share their strategies. Close in prayer, asking God to help us hold on to His promises as we wrestle with various areas of our lives.

Choose one of the areas below that you are currently wrestling with (or come up with one of your own). Then, using the accompanying Scripture passages, come up with a "wrestling strategy" to use in your struggle. After you've come up with a strategy, give that strategy a name—preferably something that sounds like a professional wrestling move (the "Flying Faith-Builder," the "Triple Truster," etc.).

Honoring Parents
Passages: Proverbs 6:20-22; Ephesians 6:1-4; James 1:19, 20

Wrestling Strategy:

Strategy Name:

Resolving Conflict with Friends
Passages: Matthew 18:15-17; Romans 13:9, 10

Wrestling Strategy:

Strategy Name:

Establishing God-Honoring Priorities
Passages: Proverbs 11:4; 19:1; Luke 16:13-15; Romans 8:5

Wrestling Strategy:

Strategy Name:

Trusting God
Passages: Psalm 46:1; Matthew 21:18-22; John 15:5

Wrestling Strategy:

Strategy Name:

Remaining Sexually Pure
Passages: I Samuel 2:22-25; Proverbs 5:1-10; Matthew 6:9-13; Romans 12:1, 2, 9, 10

Wrestling Strategy:

Strategy Name:

Other:
Passages:

Wrestling Strategy:

Strategy Name:

GENESIS 33

Home Sweet Home?

OVERVIEW

Because of God's intervention, Esau forgives and accepts Jacob. Esau wants Jacob to come with him back to their hometown, but Jacob persuades Esau to go ahead without him. Jacob builds a home for himself in a different city. Jacob has received his blessing—he has his children, his homeland, and God's protection.

OPENING ACT

(Needed: Snacks)

Think of a minor offense that your kids have committed lately (e.g., talking during last week's Bible study). Announce that the only people who will receive snacks are those who properly ask for forgiveness for the past offense. Explain that kids must write their requests for forgiveness in the form of a question. If the question is worded *exactly* right, they will receive forgiveness (and snacks); if not, they must try again. The exact wording you'll look for is "Will you please forgive me?" If any of these words are excluded or out of order on a person's request, deny him or her forgiveness. If no one words his or her request exactly right the first time, announce that the words in the request you're looking for are *me, you, will, please,* and *forgive*; then let kids try again. After a few minutes, stop the game and allow everyone to raid the snacks.

DATE I USED THIS SESSION _____ GROUP I USED IT WITH _____

NOTES FOR NEXT TIME _____

_____

_____

1. Put yourself in Jacob's position. You're returning to your homeland after twenty years to a brother, Esau, who threatened to kill you. As you approach, you see your brother coming at you with four hundred men. The only thing you have time to do is make a large sign to let Esau know how you feel. What would you write on your sign? ("I'm really sorry about the stew incident"; "Did you like the animals I sent?"; "Please don't kill me!"; "How's Mom?"; "Love your neighbor as yourself"; etc.) **Why?**

2. **Look at verse 2. Why do you think Jacob put his family in this order?** (Jacob cared most about Rachel and Joseph, and he wanted to keep them as far from harm as possible; he cared more for Leah and her children than for the maidservants and their kids.) **How do you think this made the maidservants and Leah feel? Would you have ordered them differently? If so, how?**

3. Jacob bowed down to Esau seven times as Jacob approached him (33:3). **This really wasn't necessary, since Jacob was the one who had the blessing. Why do you think Jacob did this?** (He wanted to ease Esau's anger. He knew he had received his blessing in dishonest ways and didn't want Esau to harm his family.)

4. **If you were Esau, what might you have considered doing as you saw Jacob coming toward you?** (Perhaps killing the little schemer—or at least *pretending* to be mad at him still to throw a little scare into him.)

5. Jacob was afraid that Esau wouldn't forgive him. **Do you think it's easier to forgive a family member or a friend for wronging you? Explain.**

6. **What can you learn from Jacob about how to treat someone you've wronged?** (Try to offer some kind of appeasement for your offense. Show the person deep respect. Don't try to defend your actions. Try to look to the future of your relationship instead of dwelling on the past.) **What can you learn from Esau?** (The importance of forgiveness.)

7. **Why do you think Jacob insisted that Esau accept his gifts** (33:8-11)**?** (Perhaps he really felt bad for what he had done and wanted to make amends. Perhaps he was protecting himself from being accused by Esau of being unfair.)

8. **Jacob didn't seem to want to go with Esau or to have Esau's men stay with him** (33:13-17). **Why do you think Jacob wanted to be alone with his family and possessions?** (Maybe he didn't trust Esau. Perhaps he wanted his own land. Perhaps he didn't want to share his possessions and land with Esau. Perhaps he had his own plan which didn't include Esau.)

9. **Jacob finally received the whole blessing—protection, children, and land. But it took quite a long time and quite a few trials before it happened. If you were going to write a book about the life of Jacob, what would you title it? Why?** (*A Man of Conflicts, The Man God Protected, The Scam of the Century, Son of Laughter* [an actual book about Jacob, written by Frederick Buechner], etc.)

10. **God pulled off the impossible—at least by human standards—in bringing His blessing to Jacob. What impossible situations—according to your standards—are you facing for which you'd like God's help?**

Hand out copies of the reproducible sheet, "Sorry Seems to Be the Hardest Word." After a few minutes, have kids share their responses. Then say: **These were some tough family scenarios. But think about Esau and Jacob's situation. Jacob tricked Esau out of his birthright and his blessing. In today's society, that would be like losing out on a family inheritance you were entitled to when your parents died. That's a big deal. So you can see why the tension must have been pretty thick between Esau and Jacob. But we read how God intervened in the situation, softening Esau's heart and making Jacob "sweat it out" before receiving his blessing of his promised homeland.** Close by praying that God would intervene in any conflicts between your group members and their family members or friends.

SORRY
Seems to Be the <u>**Hardest**</u> Word

In each of the following scenarios, someone has been wronged by a family member. For each situation, write down what a typical *response might be. Then write down what a* godly *response might be.*

Situation 1

Tonya is a popular junior at Franklin High School. Her brother, Wallace, is a freshman who is desperately trying to become popular too. One day while Wallace is talking with some of Tonya's friends, he mentions an old family photo album that contains some embarrassing pictures of Tonya. At the urging of the older kids, Wallace brings some of the embarrassing pictures to school. He then helps "play a little joke" on Tonya by making copies of the photos and posting them around the school. When Tonya sees the photos posted all over the hallway and lunchroom, she's mortified. She rushes home in tears.

Situation 2

Hernando wants to skip school so he can go to an afternoon baseball game with some of his friends (who are also skipping school). He knows his mother would never allow him to miss school unless he was sick, so Hernando fakes an illness. Using a warm washcloth, he makes his skin appear to be clammy and feverish. Then he gives a convincing performance of someone suffering from the chills. His mom is convinced, and forbids Hernando from going to school "in his condition."

She leaves for work, promising to return home as early as possible tonight to care for Hernando. (Hernando's mom works two jobs—one as a hotel maid in the morning, and the other as a maintenance worker in an office building in the afternoon and evening.) After lounging around the house for a few hours, Hernando leaves to join his friends at the ballpark. Meanwhile, his mother starts to worry about leaving Hernando alone. So after finishing her duties at the hotel—and after much debate—she decides to take the day off (without pay) from her second job in order to stay home with her "sick" son. When she gets home, Hernando is nowhere to be found.

GENESIS 34

Someone's Out for Vengeance for Dinah

Jacob's daughter, Dinah, catches the eye of a local man named Shechem, who apparently forces her to have sex with him and then wants to marry her. After Jacob shares the news with his sons, they contrive an elaborate and premeditated plan for revenge. Hiding their rage for Shechem's action, they actually consent to the marriage in order to convince the men of Shechem's city to be circumcised. Then, with the males of the city incapacitated, two of Jacob's sons kill them all and take their women and possessions.

Hand out copies of the reproducible sheet, "An Equal and Opposite Reaction?" Kids should consider which response might be appropriate for each offense. Encourage kids to add their own contributions to either column. Kids may discover that when they're harmed in some way, their tendency may not be to "get even." Rather, their tendency may be to try to do *worse* to the other person than has been done to them. Getting even doesn't provide quite the satisfaction that "sweet revenge" does. But this session shows how revenge can get way out of control if we allow our feelings to go unchecked.

DATE I USED THIS SESSION _____ GROUP I USED IT WITH _____

NOTES FOR NEXT TIME _____

_____

_____

1. Think of some times when people have made you feel angry, embarrassed, or hurt. Have you ever wished you could do serious harm to someone—in retaliation—if you thought you could get away with it without getting caught? Explain.

2. When Jacob's daughter, Dinah, went to visit some of the women of the land, she was seen by a young man named Shechem who forced her to have sex with him (34:1, 2). **What do you think would be an appropriate punishment for Shechem after such an offense? Would your answer change if you knew that Shechem loved Dinah very much and wanted to marry her (34:3, 4)? Why or why not?** If no one mentions it, point out that we don't know how Dinah felt about Shechem. Later in Israelite law, the violation of a virgin not yet pledged to be married required a payment to the girl's family and a marriage between the two people (Deuteronomy 22:28, 29).

3. The incident should have been prevented, but it wasn't. After it became too late to change what had happened, **what do you think the two families should have done?** Compare group members' reponses with the actual actions taken in Genesis 34:5-12.

4. Shechem and his family don't seem like terrible people. **Do you think they were making a good faith effort to settle the matter? Why or why not?** (Perhaps. But we must remember that Jacob is weathy and is a potential threat to the people of the area. They might want to ally with him and "cash in" on his wealth. [See Genesis 34:20-24.])

5. Even if Shechem and his family were being deceitful, they were up against people who were a lot better at it. **What proposal did Jacob's sons offer (34:13-17)?** (They insisted on all of the men in Shechem's family being circumcised before they would permit Dinah to marry Shechem.) **If you'd been part of Shechem's family, how would you have responded to Jacob's sons' proposal?**

6. No one in Shechem's family seemed to suspect that Jacob's sons' proposal was fishy (34:18-24). **Why do you**

suppose that was? (Perhaps Shechem was blinded by his love for Dinah. Perhaps the rest of the family were blinded by their greed for Jacob's riches.)

7. **Three days later, the real reason for Jacob's sons' request was made known as Simeon and Levi killed every male in Shechem's family (34:25-29). Do you think this was a just punishment? Explain.** (Forced sex is a horrible offense, but the retribution of mass murder seems too severe.)

8. **All of Jacob's sons seem to have been in on the plan (34:13). But only two of them carried it out, and they got in trouble—both immediately (34:30) and later when Jacob was officially blessing his sons (49:5-7). Why do you suppose the two of them were singled out?** (Planning evil is bad, but going through with it is certainly worse.)

9. **We aren't told what Dinah thought about all of this. What would you guess she might be thinking?** (Perhaps she would have preferred to marry Shechem. Now that he was dead and she was no longer a virgin, her opportunities for marriage [and, in that culture, fulfillment in life] were gone.)

10. **Why do you think Jesus placed so much emphasis on turning the other cheek, loving enemies, and not returning evil for evil?** (Matters of revenge and justice should be left up to God. When placed in our hands, the conflict almost always escalates rather than being reduced.)

Hand out paper and pencils. Ask kids to complete the following sentence: "The worst thing I ever did to get even with someone who wronged me was . . ." Don't have kids put their names on their papers, but explain that you plan to collect and read them. After you read the confessions, challenge kids to have nothing more to do with revenge or retribution. Explain that we are certain to face occasional unfair and unwanted circumstances. But when we try to create "justice" ourselves, we usually make the situation worse. Close with a prayer, asking God to help your group members become more forgiving—especially in cases in which it is difficult to do.

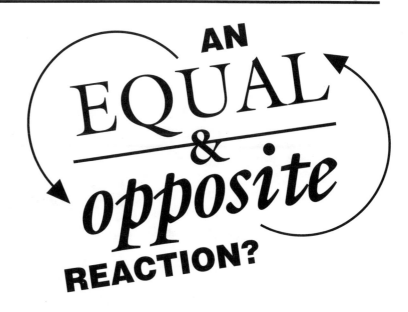

AN EQUAL & opposite REACTION?

Isaac Newton is credited with the scientific law stating that for every action, there is an equal and opposite reaction. However, that law rarely holds true when offenses and revenge are involved. (But who's to say that the action of the apple falling on Newton didn't result in his reaction of grabbing a chainsaw and making sure that particular tree never bothered him again?)

A number of offenses are listed in the left column below, and a number of responses are provided in the right column. For each of the offenses, select the response that you would be most likely to choose (if you thought you could get away with it). If you don't see anything that looks quite right, feel free to invent a response that you feel is appropriate. Remember—this isn't what you should do; it's what you would like to do.

Offenses

Someone steals your boyfriend or girlfriend.

Someone gives you the finger.

Someone starts a rumor that you are pregnant or that you got someone pregnant.

Someone intentionally destroys a possession that you hold dear.

Someone says nasty things about your mother or father.

Someone makes fun of some physical trait of yours.

Someone writes racist insults across your locker.

During gym class, someone smears heat-producing lotion in your underwear.

Someone gives you a humiliating nickname.

Someone behind you imitates your every action in a comical and embarrassing way.

Possible Responses

You publicly "de-pants" the person.

You steal his or her clothes from the locker room and force him or her to "streak" through the gym.

You get all of your friends to stop speaking to the person.

You convince a large friend to beat the tar out of the person.

You tell a teacher the person cheated on a major test.

You spread the word the person has AIDS.

You toilet paper the person's yard.

You slash the person's car tires with a knife.

You challenge the person to a fight.

You lock the person in his or her locker for several hours.

Schemers 10, Dreamers 1

OVERVIEW

God changes Jacob's name to Israel. Rachel gives birth to one more son, Benjamin, and then dies. Later, Isaac dies. The saga then shifts its focus to Joseph, Jacob's favorite son. Joseph's special attention creates jealousy among his brothers. Joseph compounds the problem by describing to his brothers his dreams of superiority. His brothers plot to kill Joseph, but they find an opportunity to sell him as a slave instead.

OPENING ACT

Divide your room into five sections: "Mother," "Father," "Sister(s)," "Brother(s)," and "Other Family Member(s)." Explain that you will read several questions. After each one, kids should move to the section that *best* answers the question. Ask: **Who would you go to first for help with schoolwork? Where would you get the best advice for planning your future? Where do you go with questions about romance and dating? Who do you think likes you best? Who are you most like?** As kids move around, listen for comments that might reveal family conflicts. Afterward, explain that family problems aren't uncommon—even among important biblical characters. Then move into your study of Joseph.

DATE I USED THIS SESSION _____ GROUP I USED IT WITH _____

NOTES FOR NEXT TIME _____

_____

_____

1. What are the things your brothers and/or sisters do that annoy you the most? How about your parents? On a scale of one to ten—with ten being the most—how serious are the conflicts and tensions between you and your brothers and/or sisters?

2. Read Genesis 37:2-11. How would you feel about Joseph if he were *your* brother? What, if anything, would you do if you had a brother who acted the way Joseph behaved around his brothers?

3. Who do you think was more responsible for the problems within the family—Jacob or Joseph? Explain. (Jacob's favoritism certainly didn't help the situation, but Joseph was responsible for his tattletale tendencies [37:2] and for broadcasting his dreams [37:5-9].)

4. Do you think this chapter describes *all* of Joseph's annoying habits or just a sampling? Explain. (Joseph's behavior must have been consistently problematic in their eyes to get to the point where his brothers wanted to *kill* him [37:12-18].)

5. Do you think Joseph's brothers were engaging in "big talk," or did they *really* want to see him dead? (Not all of them actually wanted to kill him [37:21, 22, 26, 27], but no one seemed willing to speak up for him.) **Have you ever been in a crowd that was picking on someone? Did you stand up for the person? Why or why not?**

6. What prevented Joseph's brothers from carrying out their plot to kill him (37:23-28)? (A caravan came by, giving them the opportunity to sell Joseph, instead of killing him.) **What does this "coincidence" tell you about the way God works?** (God is responsible for more "coincidences" than we'll ever know.)

7. How do you think Joseph's brothers felt about their decision after they'd sold Joseph? Why? (At least one of them experienced guilt immediately [37:29, 30]. Many years later they all thought of themselves as co-conspirators in a horrible crime [42:21]. And as soon as they got home they would begin to witness their father's intense grief.) **What does this tell you making decisions "in the heat of the moment"?**

8. The brothers' action against Joseph quickly escalated into an ongoing deceit against Jacob (37:31-35). Can you think of a time when you did something wrong, and then had to do a lot of other wrong things to keep from being discovered? If so, what happened? Are you trying to keep anything hidden *right now*?

9. Joseph ended up in Egypt (37:36)—a long way from home in days of camel transportation. How do you think he felt? (Perhaps he was worried about what the future held for him. Perhaps he was afraid that he'd never see his father again. Perhaps he was angry at his brothers for putting him in this situation.)

10. At this point in the story, would you expect anything good to come from Joseph's life? Why or why not? After several group members have responded, point out that just as they shouldn't be too quick to give up on Joseph, they also should be patient during their own turbulent teenage years.

It's common for young people to focus more on what's going wrong in their lives than on what's going right. But when we compare ourselves to Joseph, we may discover that we don't have nearly as much to complain about. Give your group members the opportunity to write their own stories by completing the reproducible sheet, "My Bio." After a few volunteers read what they have written, challenge everyone to be more willing to endure a few sufferings and less quick to complain when wronged by siblings (or to cause *them* unnecessary suffering). Explain that the most important part of each person's life is the part that is yet to come. What we've suffered in the past can be left in the past. If we want our lives to get better, we have to focus on the future, remain faithful to God, and get a little closer to Him each day. That's the only way we'll ever have truly successful lives.

My Bio

Joseph had a sad story, but then, don't we all? Your story has been started below, but we need you to fill in a few final facts. Then compare your past to Joseph's and see what the two of you might have in common.

MY STORY, by _____

I was **b o r n** _____ years ago in a **p l a c e** called _____. Everyone agreed that I was a _____ baby. But then, those were carefree days of innocence.

Later, as I was growing up, I had _____ **b r o t h e r s** and _____ **s i s t e r s.** When it came to getting along with each other, most of the time we _____. But there were a few times when we really _____. I remember one particular incident where my parent(s) did something that caused some real problems. What they did was _____ _____, which resulted in _____ _____. But to be completely honest, I can't **b l a m e** everything on my parents. For example, there was that time when I decided to _____. Before everyone got over that little incident, I thought we were going to _____.

Right now, the big family **c o n f l i c t** in my life is _____. I'm pretty sure it can be worked out. But first I **n e e d** to _____. Then _____ needs to _____. And finally, **G O D** needs to _____.

My family has a lot of faults. But, on the **p o s i t i v e** side, my parents are _____ _____, my brothers and sisters are _____ _____, and my wish for our future as a family is that we _____ _____.

GENESIS 39–41

Egypped

After being sold by his brothers and taken to Egypt, Joseph is placed in a home where the wife of a prominent official lusts after him. Determined to remain loyal to God, Joseph refuses her sexual advances. Consequently, she falsely accuses him of attempted rape. Joseph is thrown in prison. In prison, he helps two cellmates and is promised help in return. However, years go by before he gets out of prison. After Joseph is released, his God-given wisdom is immediately recognized, and he becomes second-in-command over all of Egypt.

As a group, write a story about Bad-Breaks Bradley. Your goal should be to see exactly how vivid a "worst-case scenario" you can create. The first person might begin by saying, "Bradley works as a custodian at the School of the Perpetually Nauseated. You can imagine his job description. But Bradley thinks, *No matter. This is the worst that can happen to me.* But he's wrong because . . ." Then the person passes the story to the next person, who will add another sad chapter to Bradley's saga. Keep adding to the story as long as you can. By the end of the story, Bradley should have earned the sympathy of your kids. Then move into the story of Joseph, which may make Bradley's life seem rosy in comparison.

DATE I USED THIS SESSION _____ GROUP I USED IT WITH _____

NOTES FOR NEXT TIME _____

_____

_____

1. Have you ever had a day or a week in which absolutely nothing went right? If so, tell us about it. What did you do to deserve such a lousy experience?

2. When last we heard about Joseph, he was seventeen (37:2) and had been sold by his brothers as a slave headed for Egypt (37:28). If you were in his place, how optimistic would you be that your life would turn out OK? How well did Joseph cope with the situation (39:1-6)? Why? (Joseph had left home, but God never left Joseph. Even when Joseph was a slave, God caused him to prosper, which pleased Joseph's owner.)

3. How difficult do you think it was for Joseph to resist the sexual temptations of Potiphar's wife (39:6-12)? Why? (Even if Joseph wasn't sexually attracted to her, he still had to know that rejecting her advances could eventually get him in trouble. After all, it's not like he could sue her for sexual harrassment.)

4. Why do you think God allowed Joseph to suffer for doing the right thing? (God's plan was for Joseph to be over *all* of Egypt, not just Potiphar's household. All would *eventually* be made clear, though at the time, it must have been a severe disappointment for Joseph.)

5. If you'd been in Joseph's position, after his experiences with his brothers and in Potiphar's household, what might have been your attitude in prison? Would you have preferred to get involved in prison life or would you have preferred solitary confinement? Explain. Compare kids' responses with Joseph's actual actions in Genesis 39:20-23.

6. How much positive influence can a person have in prison? (If the person remains faithful to God, quite a bit.) Review the story of the baker and the cupbearer (Genesis 40) to show how much (and why) Joseph was respected.

7. How would you feel if you did someone a huge favor and asked for a small favor in return, only to have the person forget all about you? Why? See Genesis 40:12-15, 23.

8. After two more years, Joseph finally had an opportunity to get out of jail. He had one shot at gaining Pharaoh's favor. When Pharoah said, "I hear you can help me" (paraphrase of 41:15), **what would you have said? Why?** (Some people might say whatever they thought Pharaoh wanted to hear if it would be to their advantage. But Joseph made it completely clear that his wisdom came from God [41:16].)

9. After Joseph correctly interpreted Pharaoh's dream and gave him some good advice, why wasn't he returned to his cell? (It became obvious to Pharaoh that Joseph wasn't just an ordinary guy. And since Joseph had spoken so clearly for God, Pharaoh wanted to have Joseph's God on his side [41:37-40].)

10. How long had Joseph been struggling to be understood and accepted by other people? (About thirteen years [Genesis 37:2; 41:46].) Do you ever feel misunderstood and unaccepted by other people? If so, do you think God can use that to His—and your—benefit? How?

11. Would you be willing to go through everything Joseph experienced if you knew you would come out rich and famous by the time you're thirty? Why or why not? Since you have no such promise, how do you usually handle unfair situations in which you have to suffer a little? Why?

The reproducible sheet, "Worst Case Scenario," asks kids to list the worst possible things they can think of in a number of categories. Then they are asked to consider what they might do if all of those "worst possible" things happened to them at the same time. Discuss kids' responses. Then explain that when people remain faithful to God, He oversees their future. While occasional suffering is part of everyone's life, God is still in control. Even if a Christian's life is a disappointment, his or her *eternal* life won't be. Read I Peter 4:12-16. Then close with a prayer for patience to endure current sufferings in order to experience the future blessings of God.

Worst-Case
SCENARIO

You think your life is bad now? It could get worse, you know. For each of the following categories, think of the absolute worst things you can. Write down your answers and be ready to compare them with everyone else's.

What would be the worst possible . . .

Job? _____

Place to live? _____

Type of pet? _____

Disease/medical condition? _____

Style of clothing? _____

Food? _____

Dessert? _____

Hair style? _____

Weather? _____

Music style? _____

TV show(s)? _____

Household chores? _____

Hobby? _____

Neighbor? _____

Sight from your bedroom window? _____

Homework subject/assignment? _____

Now suppose for a moment that you lived in a place where all of the worst possible things you've listed come true. You are taking the classes, doing the chores, eating the food, and experiencing everything else you just described. What would be your outlook on life? Why?

How often, how loudly, and to whom would you complain about your circumstances? Do you think your complaints would do any good? Why or why not?

How desperate would you be to change things? What kinds of things would you try? If a person from a strange eastern religion promised your life would get a lot better if you converted, would you try it? Why or why not?

What would you tend to think about yourself if every single thing you enjoyed or appreciated seemed to disappear as your life fell apart?

GENESIS 42–50

A Dream Come True

A famine in Canaan drives Jacob's sons to Egypt for food. Little do they know that Joseph is now governor of the whole country. Since they don't recognize him, but he knows them, Joseph can test his brothers to see if they've changed. Eventually, the entire family is reunited and settles in Egypt. Later, Joseph takes his sons to be blessed by Jacob. Instead of giving priority to Manasseh, the firstborn, Jacob reveals that Ephraim, the younger son, will be greater than his brother. After blessing his own sons, Jacob dies and is buried with Abraham and Isaac. Years later, Joseph dies.

(Needed: A tray filled with various items)

Place the following items on a tray: a bag of rice (or some other grain), silver coins, a cloth bag, a rope, lip balm, honey, pistachio nuts, almonds, a bottle of perfume, spices, a card with the name "Ben" written on it, a silver cup, and a plastic donkey. Bring out the tray and let kids look at the items for thirty seconds. Then cover up the tray and have kids write down as many of the items as they can remember. See who can recall the most items. During the Bible study, have kids pay attention to how the various items on the tray fit into the story of Joseph's reunion with his brothers.

DATE I USED THIS SESSION _____ GROUP I USED IT WITH _____

NOTES FOR NEXT TIME _____

_____

_____

1. Can you think of something you did a long time ago that you still feel guilty about? Can you recall offenses other people committed against *you*? If so, why do you think the feelings haven't gone away yet?

2. After thirteen years of suffering at the hands of your eleven brothers—suffering that included being thrown in a hole, sold into slavery, accused of rape, and a prison term—what would you do if you found yourself in a position where you had complete power over them? What did Joseph do (42:1-20)? (He accused them of being spies and put them in a precarious position to see if they would "sell out" Benjamin as they had done him.)

3. To what did the brothers attribute their misfortune (42:21-23)? (They thought they were being punished for harming Joseph.) This is *thirteen years later.* Do you think everything that went wrong still reminded them of their previous sin? Explain.

4. Joseph arranged to give them the grain they needed, but he secretly returned their money as well, which frightened them. How did he know he was going to see them again (42:24-38)? (He kept Simeon until they brought Benjamin to Egypt.) What thoughts were probably going through Simeon's mind?

5. Joseph's plan almost backfired. Jacob seemed willing to sacrifice Simeon rather than risk losing Benjamin (42:36-38). What changed his mind? (Continuation of the famine in Canaan.) If you were a parent, how do you think it would feel to have to decide which of your children might have to die? Do you think that as a parent, you will have favorites among your children? Why or why not?

6. Another test took place as the brothers started home. Joseph's personal cup, which had been planted in Benjamin's sack of grain, was "discovered" during a search. It would have been convenient for the brothers to leave Benjamin behind and move on safely. But what did they do instead? See Genesis 44:10-34. What do you think *you* would have done?

7. Joseph could no longer keep his identity hidden. The brothers were scared silly to see who they were dealing with. But why didn't Joseph do anything to get even (45:1-11)? (He realized that God was behind everything. When you see that you're part of God's plan, why hold a grudge?)

8. Soon the whole family was back together again in Egypt (45:16-18; 47:5, 6). Jacob eventually died there (49:29–50:14). But Joseph made it clear that his descendants wouldn't remain in Egypt forever (50:22-26). What strange request did he make—and why? (He made plans for his bones to be carried out of Egypt because he wanted to be buried in the land that had been promised to his family.)

9. When Jacob died, Joseph's brothers were afraid that Joseph might then try to get even with them (50:15-21)? Why didn't he? (He truly believed that God had been at work all along, so he was quick to forgive them.)

10. What can we learn from Joseph about revenge? (God can work just as easily through our sufferings as through our good times, so we should leave any retribution to Him.)

Joseph learned from his bad experiences. He was able to see that sometimes, when things go wrong, it is because "God intended it for good" (50:20). Many Bible stories bear out this truth. The reproducible sheet, "Who Woulda Thunk It?" asks group members to identify a number of more current examples of people who overcame various obstacles to succeed in life. (The people described are [1] David Letterman; [2] Sally Ride; [3] Michael Jordan; [4] George Washington Carver; [5] Helen Keller; [6] Charles Colson; [7] Franklin Roosevelt; [8] Danny DeVito; [9] Martin Luther King, Jr.; and [10] Cindy Crawford.) People have overcome gender, racial, physical, and other kinds of obstacles to make valuable contributions to the world. With God's help, your group members should be able to do an even better job of coping. Close the session in prayer, asking God to help your group members not to give up when things don't go their way.

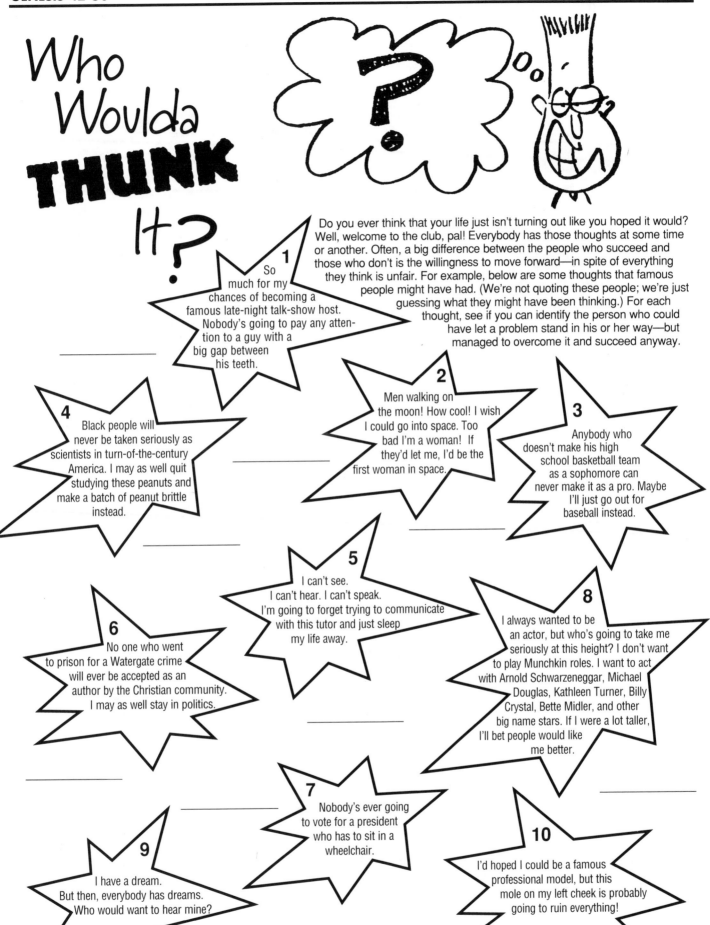

Who Woulda THUNK It?

Do you ever think that your life just isn't turning out like you hoped it would? Well, welcome to the club, pal! Everybody has those thoughts at some time or another. Often, a big difference between the people who succeed and those who don't is the willingness to move forward—in spite of everything they think is unfair. For example, below are some thoughts that famous people might have had. (We're not quoting these people; we're just guessing what they might have been thinking.) For each thought, see if you can identify the person who could have let a problem stand in his or her way—but managed to overcome it and succeed anyway.

1 So much for my chances of becoming a famous late-night talk-show host. Nobody's going to pay any attention to a guy with a big gap between his teeth.

2 Men walking on the moon! How cool! I wish I could go into space. Too bad I'm a woman! If they'd let me, I'd be the first woman in space.

3 Anybody who doesn't make his high school basketball team as a sophomore can never make it as a pro. Maybe I'll just go out for baseball instead.

4 Black people will never be taken seriously as scientists in turn-of-the-century America. I may as well quit studying these peanuts and make a batch of peanut brittle instead.

5 I can't see. I can't hear. I can't speak. I'm going to forget trying to communicate with this tutor and just sleep my life away.

6 No one who went to prison for a Watergate crime will ever be accepted as an author by the Christian community. I may as well stay in politics.

7 Nobody's ever going to vote for a president who has to sit in a wheelchair.

8 I always wanted to be an actor, but who's going to take me seriously at this height? I don't want to play Munchkin roles. I want to act with Arnold Schwarzeneggar, Michael Douglas, Kathleen Turner, Billy Crystal, Bette Midler, and other big name stars. If I were a lot taller, I'll bet people would like me better.

9 I have a dream. But then, everybody has dreams. Who would want to hear mine?

10 I'd hoped I could be a famous professional model, but this mole on my left cheek is probably going to ruin everything!

EXODUS 1–2

Born to Be Niled

OVERVIEW

It's been four hundred years since Jacob's family settled in Egypt. The Egyptians are beginning to feel threatened by the number of Israelites in their country. A new king comes to power who orders that the Israelites be made slaves. When that doesn't eliminate the problem, the Pharaoh tries to kill all newborn Israelite males. Moses' mother devises a method of ensuring her child's safety. When Moses gets older, however, he jeopardizes his position and has to flee the country.

OPENING ACT

Hand out copies of the reproducible sheet, "This Could Be a Problem." Let kids work in pairs to complete the sheet. (The answers are as follows: [1] 1,994 dollars are worth $1 more than 1,993 dollars; [2] Once—after that, it must be subtracted from 20; [3] When it's 11 o'clock and you add two hours, it's one; [4] Twenty; [5] The rope is attached to the horse, but not to anything else; [6] The man is playing baseball; he sees the umpire and the other team's catcher; [7] Stand back-to-back. [The puzzles are from "MindTrap," Great American Puzzle Factory, Inc., under license from MindTrap Games, Inc. © 1991.]) Afterward, explain that we may face problems that seem insurmountable, but a little thought and effort (and God's help) can usually show us ways around the problem. Such was the case for Moses' family.

DATE I USED THIS SESSION _____ GROUP I USED IT WITH _____

NOTES FOR NEXT TIME _____

_____

_____

1. Describe a time when a person in a position of influence over you was replaced by someone else, causing you to be affected in a strong way—either positively or negatively. (Perhaps a teacher was replaced and interest in learning rose considerably. A new coach might make love of sports disappear altogether. A stepparent can drastically affect someone's life one way or another.)

2. As the Book of Exodus begins, what changes are taking place in Egypt? See Exodus 1. *Why do you think these things were happening?* (The various sufferings experienced by the Israelites would eventually be God's way of resettling them in the promised land. [Otherwise, why would they ever *want* to leave to Egypt?])

3. Do you think the Israelites rejoiced to see that God was at work? Why or why not? (When things don't go our way, we tend to complain first and look for God's will later. We should learn from this story not to be so quick to whine.)

4. What are your feelings toward civil disobedience? Do you think it's ever appropriate to disobey the law? If so, when? (Everyone is to "submit himself to the governing authorities" [Romans 13:1]. But as the Israelite midwives realized, when the king's law contradicts God's law, we should obey the higher authority—God.)

5. If you think the problems on the handout were tough, imagine being a parent who had to figure out how to keep a child from dying (2:1-3). What methods might you have come up with for hiding children?

6. Why didn't Moses' parents just leave everything in God's hands? Why did Miriam follow the basket down the river (2:4)? (The entire Book of Exodus is filled with examples of how God used people to accomplish His plan. We are to have faith in Him, sure, but we are to also to take responsible action whenever appropriate.)

7. Imagine placing a little baby in a picnic basket and floating him down the Mississippi or any other large river. What do you suppose would be his chances of being safely

rescued? What does this story tell you about how God works? (With God in charge, Moses was not only safe, he landed at the exact time and place that Pharaoh's daughter was present [2:5-10].)

8. Moses was brought up by Pharaoh's daughter. So why do you think he identified more with the Israelites (2:11, 12)? (Perhaps his mother's influence was very strong. Or maybe God began to deal with him at an early age.)

9. We know now that God was going to use Moses to lead the Israelites out of Egypt. So why would He allow events to take place that would lead Moses *away* from Egypt (2:14, 15)? Couldn't He have saved some time by having Moses confront Pharaoh right away? (Perhaps, but Moses was not yet ready. He needed some "quiet time" first.)

10. Moses was forty at this time [Acts 7:23]. Based on the events described in Exodus 2:15-22, what do you think he assumed the rest of his life would be like? What do you think the rest of the Israelites expected (2:23)?

11. What do you suppose the rest of *your* life will be like? Do you expect any major surprises? Explain.

Close with two activities. First, in response to Moses' parents' plan to save Moses' life, have each person create his or her personal "Plan for Safety While Living in a Sinful World." This should be a list of things he or she can do to ensure that he or she doesn't fall prey to harmful influences in the world. Then have kids make a "Great Expectations List" of the things they would like God to do for them, even if their desires seem too much to hope for. (These shouldn't be fanciful whims—a new car, a million dollars, etc. Rather, the lists should include serious items—a good college in spite of low income, to become a loving parent even though one's own parents were abusive, etc.) Finally, explain that the activities are related. If we remain faithful to God while in a sinful world, we may still suffer—but God *will* reward us (though in His perfect timing, and not according to our own schedules).

This Could Be a PROBLEM

You like for people to think you're pretty smart, right? Well, let's see if you're right. Below are a few things for you to explain or figure out. If you get them all correct, maybe people will start to believe you. But even if you get three or more, you're doing pretty well.

1. 1994 American dollar bills are worth a little more than 1993 dollar bills. Why**?**

2. How many times can you subtract the number 5 from 25**?**

3. When can you add two to eleven and get one as the correct answer**?**

4. When you write down all of the numbers between 1 and 100, how many times will you write the number 9**?**

5. A horse is tied to a five-foot rope in front of a barn. A big pile of hay is six feet away. Without breaking the rope, the horse is able to eat the hay whenever it wants to. How is this possible**?**

6.. A man left home one morning. He ran for a while, then he turned left. After awhile, he turned left again, running faster than ever. Then he turned left once more and decided to go home. In the distance, he could see two masked men. Who were they**?**

7. How can you physically stand behind your best friend while he or she is standing behind you**?**

EXODUS 3–4

May I Please Be Excused?

While "on the lam" in Midian, Moses is confronted by God. Speaking from a burning bush, the Lord begins to prepare Moses to return to Egypt. Moses is reluctant at first. He gives excuse after excuse for why God should look elsewhere for a leader, but God deals with every excuse. Eventually Moses returns to Egypt and begins to be accepted by the Israelites.

Conduct an "Excuse-a-Thon." Announce that you are seeking volunteers to help with a major (and dreaded) chore such as painting the church, shoveling out barns, etc. Explain that you don't need everyone, so you'll take the people who are first to run out of good excuses. Also make it clear that no two people will be allowed to give the same excuse. Go from person to person, listening to excuses. If everyone gives a different excuse, go around again until group members begin to run out of unused excuses. Keep going as time permits to see who are the best excuse-givers.

DATE I USED THIS SESSION _____ GROUP I USED IT WITH _____

NOTES FOR NEXT TIME _____

_____

_____

1. What's the strangest thing you've ever seen in your life? UFOs? Meteors? A solar eclipse? Your little sister?

2. Moses saw a lot of strange things during his lifetime, but one of the first was a bush that looked like it was on fire, yet didn't burn up. It was also a *talking* bush (3:1-4). If you were in the middle of the wilderness by yourself and a bush started calling your name, what would you do?

3. Why do you think God didn't appear in all of His glory? Why did He "disguise" Himself (3:4-6)? (Moses was afraid enough of the voice and the burning bush. God was kind not to overwhelm him any further.)

4. God's message came as a good news-bad news announcement to Moses. What was the good news? (God would rescue His people from Egypt and lead them to the promised land.) What was the bad news—from Moses' perspective? (God was going to use Moses to do it.) When spreading the Gospel—the good news—today, do you consider any of God's expectations for you to be "bad news"? If so, in what ways? Be specific.

5. Moses had no shortage of excuses. But then, God had no shortage of solutions to each excuse Moses raised. What was Moses' first excuse (3:11)? ("I'm not important enough to work for You.") Do you ever feel that way? What was God's answer to Moses—and you (3:12)? What does it mean that God will be with you? (God is always there to support us, whether or not we are aware of His presence.)

6. What was Moses' second excuse (3:13)? ("I don't know Your name.") How did God reply (3:14)? ("I am who I am.") Are you ever confused as to what to call God? Based on your current needs, what would you like God to be for you? (A provider? A protector? A friend? A counselor?)

7. What was Moses' third excuse (4:1)? ("No one will believe me.") In response, God gave him some impressive signs to help convince people (4:2-9). You may not be able to change sticks to snakes or create instant leprosy, but do you have other signs to show that God is active in your life? (Answered prayer? The presence of the Holy Spirit? Peace during incredibly trying times?)

8. On to Moses' fourth excuse: "My speech, it ain't too terribly good. My twongue gets tisted" (4:10). God's reply was, essentially, "I created you, so I know exactly what you're capable of doing" (4:11, 12). Do you ever try to get out of doing something you know God wants you to do, using personal incompetence as an excuse? If so, do you think it's a valid excuse? Why or why not? (Public prayer? Giving a testimony to others? Missions work?)

9. Finally, Moses asked God to send someone else to do it (4:13). By this time, God was getting angry. Yet He allowed Moses to take his brother along to speak for him (4:14-17). Do you ever look for other people with which to share your spiritual responsibilities? If so, why?

10. After all of Moses' resistance, how do you think things worked out when he finally obeyed God (4:27-31)? (The first response of the people of Israel, during this time when Moses was so unsure of himself, was very positive.)

11. Would you prefer a life with no major sufferings if it meant you would have no major thrills or accomplishments either? Or are you willing to risk occasional suffering if the likely result is significant spiritual and emotional growth? Do you think you get to choose which way you live? Explain. (While we are not in control of the results, we do choose how often and how far to "go out on a limb" in faith. The bolder we become, the more likely we are to experience rejection or failure in some cases, but deeper spiritual fulfillment overall.)

The reproducible sheet, "Snakes Give Me the Shakes," challenges kids to identify and evaluate their fears. When they finish, discuss how their fears may lessen their effectiveness as Christians—either directly or indirectly. Then close with a prayer for courage to overcome the fears that hold kids back from being the complete people that God wants them to be.

Snakes
Give Me the Shakes

When Moses wanted to be sure that other people could tell God was active in his life, God gave him a sign. Moses threw his staff on the ground and it became a snake (Exodus 4:3). Upon seeing this, Moses did what any intelligent person would do—he ran! But God told him to pick it up—not behind the head where, if you have to touch a snake at all, is the best place to do it, but rather by the tail. And somehow Moses found the faith and courage to obey.

The snakes below represent *your* fears: dentists, not being liked, public speaking, claustrophobia, death of a loved one, or whatever. The bigger the snake, the bigger the fear. So rate your top five fears (by size). Then list any ways you can think of that each particular fear might affect you as a Christian. If time permits, also try to think of some good ways to handle the fear and not let it prevent you from doing the things you want and need to do.

EXODUS 5–10

Dark and Froggy, with Occasional Hail

OVERVIEW

Moses confronts Pharaoh about Israel's release, but the Egyptian king isn't eager to lose such a large slave force. The more Moses does what God tells him to do, the more the Israelites seem to suffer. God performs incredible miracles to change Pharaoh's mind, and Pharaoh temporarily relents after each one. But when everything goes back to normal, Pharaoh again becomes hard-hearted and refuses to grant Moses' request.

OPENING ACT

(Needed: Prepared index cards)

Before the session, write each of the first nine plagues of Egypt (Exodus 7–10) on a separate index card. The plagues are as follows: blood, frogs, gnats, flies, the death of livestock, boils, hail, locusts, and darkness. One at a time, have volunteers come to the front of the room, draw a card, and act out that plague (using pantomime) for the rest of the group to guess. Continue until all of the plagues have been acted out. Then ask volunteers to arrange the plagues in order of severity. When they're finished, ask them to explain why they arranged the cards as they did.

DATE I USED THIS SESSION _____ GROUP I USED IT WITH _____

NOTES FOR NEXT TIME _____

_____

_____

1. What's the best way for someone to convince you to do something you don't want to do? Do you respond better to being asked nicely or to "arm twisting"? Why?

2. If it was your responsibility to rescue a small nation being held as slaves by one of the most powerful countries in the world, how would you go about doing it? Compare group members' responses with Moses' actions. Point out that Moses started with a polite request (Exodus 5:1-3).

3. But Pharaoh wasn't about to let thousands of slaves just walk away. In fact, he decided to make the Israelites work even harder (5:4-19). How do you think that made the Israelites feel about Moses (5:20, 21)? How do you think that made Moses feel about God (5:22, 23)?

4. Of course God knew that Pharaoh would turn down Moses' request. So why do you think God had Moses ask something when He already knew what the answer was going to be (6:1-12)? (By allowing Pharaoh to stubbornly refuse request after request, God was eventually going to show him who was really in charge of world events. When the Israelites left Egypt, everyone would know *for sure* that God was responsible for their deliverance.)

5. In fact, God made it clear to Moses that Pharaoh *wouldn't* cooperate, but that the eventual outcome of the situation was already certain (6:28–7:7). Yet in the meantime, Moses still had to endure a lot of rejection from Pharaoh. Have you ever been in a similar situation? If your group members practice love-your-enemies, turn-the-other-cheek Christianity, perhaps they can relate to Moses' situation. Even when we know we're right and what the outcome is going to be, rejection is no fun.

6. Asking nicely didn't work, so Moses and Aaron used signs from God to try to change Pharaoh's mind (7:8-13). When that didn't work either, God sent a series of plagues. List these plagues in the order that they occurred. ([1] The Nile and other water sources becoming bloody and undrinkable [7:14-24]; [2] Frogs overrunning the land [8:1-15]; [3] Gnats everywhere [8:16-19]; [4] Dense swarms of flies [8:20-32]; [5] A killing disease that destroyed the Egyptian livestock [9:1-7]; [6] Terrible boils on all Egyptians [9:8-12]; [7] Hail unlike anything ever seen before in Egypt [9:13-35]; [8] Crop-destroying locusts [10:1-20]; [9] Total and ongoing darkness [10:21-29].) **If you were Pharaoh, at what point do you think you might have given in? Why do you think he didn't?**

7. If you were an Egyptian citizen during the time of the plagues, how do you think you would feel about Pharaoh? How would you feel about Israel's God?

8. What tactics did Pharaoh use to dismiss the plagues? (At first, he tried to explain away God's miracles [7:11-13, 21-23]. Later, it seems that he tried to pretend the events hadn't taken place—or that they weren't as bad as they actually were [8:15, 19, 32; 9:12, 34]. He also tried compromise [10:10, 11, 24].) **How do some people try to use similar tactics today in response to spiritual matters?**

9. Why do you think God didn't just strike Pharaoh down and let His people walk out of Egypt? (Perhaps He was teaching them some lessons about trusting Him.)

10. God spared His people from much of the suffering that resulted from the plagues (8:22; 9:6, 26; 10:23). **Do you think He still spares His people from suffering today? If so, how? Why do you think God sometimes allows people to face suffering?**

The reproducible sheet, "A Pox on You," asks kids to think of plagues to inflict on people who annoy them. When they finish, make a serious point. Have them consider how many of the people they listed might refuse to change their minds— no matter what happened (due to stubbornness or whatever). Point out that Pharaoh faced unnecessary suffering because he refused to give in to God's will. Similarly, we may suffer when we insist on our own way rather than seeking what God wants. Close with a prayer of submission to God. Challenge kids to remain submissive to Him.

Have you ever wished you had unlimited power—just for a while? When people are picking on you mercilessly, have you ever wanted to freeze them in their tracks just long enough to dress them as Pilgrims? To change them into donkeys (or the animal of your choice)? To put their heads on backwards?

HERE'S YOUR CHANCE. Don't use names, but in the left column below, list the things that people have done to you recently for which you'd like to get even somehow. Then, in the right column, create a suitable "plague" that you think would get each person's attention. Be creative.

OFFENSES AGAINST ME	WHAT I MIGHT DO IF I COULD

When you finish with the previous part of the sheet, go through your list and try to predict whether or not each plague would convince the person to apologize and start being nice to you. Or would it make the person even more stubborn and hostile toward you?

EXODUS 11:1–12:30

The Consequences of Unbelief

OVERVIEW

So far, nine terrible plagues haven't succeeded in convincing Pharaoh to let the Israelites leave Egypt. But God is about to demonstrate how severe the consequences can be for refusing to comply with His commands. He gives clear instructions as well as consequences. If His instructions are followed, no harm will come. But in every household where His command is ignored, the firstborn will die. Knowing that this will be the event that finally changes Pharaoh's mind, God also prepares Moses and the Israelites for a quick departure from Egypt.

OPENING ACT

Hand out copies of the reproducible sheet, "Preventive Maintenance." Give kids a few minutes to complete the sheet. When they finish, ask: **How much time do you spend each day in prayer and Bible study, trying to stay close to God in order to prevent temptation or sin?** Perhaps some kids will discover that they are devoting more time to *physical* preventive maintainance than to *spiritual* preparation. This session will show how little effort was needed to prevent God's judgment, yet how important it was to make that small bit of effort.

DATE I USED THIS SESSION _____ GROUP I USED IT WITH _____

NOTES FOR NEXT TIME _____

_____

_____

1. When was the last time you got in serious trouble for disobeying or ignoring a clear instruction of someone in authority? Why didn't you obey? What happened as a result? How did you get back in the person's good graces?

2. After nine plagues, Pharaoh still had the title of king, but many of the Egyptians were more inclined to listen to Moses (11:1-3). **Why was that?** (Moses spoke with God's authority—not only for the present, but for what would happen in the future as well.) **Do you think that principle still holds true today? Why or why not?** (Many people today put more faith in the words of Christian leaders than in the words of elected or appointed officials.)

3. Everything Moses had predicted had come true. So when he said that the firstborn of every single Egyptian household was going to die (11:4-8), **why do you think Pharaoh didn't take action?** (We are told that "the Lord hardened Pharaoh's heart" [11:10]. Apparently Pharaoh had hardened his own heart so often that God confirmed his callous attitude until the painful judgment of this tenth plague. Anyone with a casual disregard for God's Word places himself or herself in the same vulnerable position. Confession, repentance, and obedience are much more preferable.)

4. Read Exodus 12:1-16. **Put yourself in the place of an Israelite child as the nation prepared for its first Passover. How do you think you would feel? What questions would you have?**

5. **Why is the event called "Passover"** (12:12, 13)**?** (Because in any house where the blood was applied, God would "pass over" and do no harm.)

6. **Why was the celebration of Passover to be continued** (12:14-20)**?** (Much as Christians celebrate the Lord's Supper, it is an ongoing reminder for what God has done for His people.) **Why don't most Christians still celebrate Passover?** (Jesus' crucifixion was at Passover, which is a distinctly Jewish celebration. We celebrate His *permanent* victory over sin and death.) Point out the symbolism of Christ's crucifixion—a perfect sacrifice, the importance of the blood, salvation from death, etc.

7. **How do you usually feel at the sight of blood? Why?** (Most of us are removed from the slaughter of animals today. We think of blood as unpleasant or even disgusting.) **How does it make you feel to know that the shedding of blood is a basis of your faith? Why?**

8. Read Exodus 12:29, 30. **How does it make you feel to know that God would not only allow such a harsh judgment, but would *initiate* it as well?**

9. **In what ways do people tend to take their faith for granted today?** If no one mentions it, point out that it's easy to memorize and quote Romans 6:23 ("The wages of sin is death") without giving it much thought. But we should give the matter a *lot* of thought. We should be abundantly thankful for God's sacrificial provision of salvation.

10. **What are some things you can do to keep from taking your faith for granted in the future? Is there anything you can do on a regular basis—weekly, monthly, or annually—to remember the things God has done for you?**

Suggest that one reason we may tend to take our faith too lightly is that we overlook the "little things" we should be doing. Splashing blood on the doorposts was a simple chore; yet the completion of the task meant the difference between death and life. To wrap up the session, have kids name every command they can recall from Scripture. Point out that God has given us these commands for our own good. From our inward relationship with Him comes our desire to obey His rules. If your kids have trouble getting past the Ten Commandments, challenge them to get a little more involved in Scripture in the near future. If you accumulate a long list of things you know you should do, encourage kids to take those "little" things (honesty, humility, servanthood, and so forth) more seriously. It will make the difference between a faith that is alive and thriving, and one that is dead or dying.

Preventive Maintenance

We like for our lives to **run smoothly**, so we may try to do whatever it takes to avoid unpleasant things. For each of the things listed below, **estimate** how much **time** each day (on average) you spend trying to prevent it. Then give some specifics for exactly how you go about trying to keep it from **happening.**

When You Try to Avoid...	What Things Do You Do to Avoid It?	How Much Time Do You Spend on It?
Unpleasant odors from various parts of the body		
Zits		
Getting out of shape		
A bad-hair day		
Looking like a nerd		
Tooth decay		
Failing in school		
Getting bored		
Feeling lonely		

EXODUS 12:31–14:31

The Red Sea Strolls

While the first nine plagues hadn't convinced Pharaoh to release the Israelites, the deaths of all of the firstborn males finally does. Thanks to God's advance instructions, the Israelites are ready to go. They even carry much of the wealth of the Egyptians with them. God's presence is clearly visible at all times. However, Pharaoh soon regrets his decision and sends his army to retrieve the Israelites. God miraculously parts the Red Sea to allow the Israelites to walk through on dry land—and brings the waters back down on the pursuing Egyptians.

Begin the session with a game of "Chase the Caterpillar's Tail." Have group members line up single file. Instruct each person to place his or her hands on the waist of the person in front of him or her. Group members should hold firmly and not let go. The goal is for the person at the front of the line to grab the last person in line. The back person, of course, should try to keep from being caught. Use this activity to introduce the subject of pursuit. The Egyptian army's pursuit of the Israelites through the Red Sea is one of the most thrilling stories in the Bible.

DATE I USED THIS SESSION _____ GROUP I USED IT WITH _____

NOTES FOR NEXT TIME _____

_____

_____

1. Describe what you think would be the ideal lifestyle—location, job, hobbies, and so forth. Now suppose you had everything just the way you described, but weren't completely free. For instance, what if you had it all in a minimum security prison where you had to check in with someone regularly and couldn't do everything exactly *when* you wanted to? How would you feel? Why?

2. The Israelites had settled in Egypt with complete freedom and everything they could ask for (Genesis 47:11, 12). This situation eventually threatened the Egyptians and led to Israel's slavery. But now the Israelites were free again. Why do you think everyone was so eager for the Israelites to leave (Exodus 12:31-33)? (People were afraid they might die if the Israelites remained.)

3. The Israelites had been in Egypt for 430 years (12:40). Their original group had numbered seventy people (Genesis 46:27). By now, how many would you guess there were? (According to Exodus 12:37, there were 600,000 men, plus women and children.)

4. Put yourself in Moses' place. You've just been blamed for killing off all of the oldest male children in Egypt. You finally have permission to leave, but there's nowhere to go except the desert. You're leading a million people, with their animals and possessions. It's the middle of the night. How would you like to have that job? Why? What do you think would be your top three problems or priorities?

5. In addition to everything else, God asked Moses to consecrate all of the firstborn males in Israel to Him (13:1-16). Why do you think He chose that particular time for a little ceremony? (The firstborn males were the ones who had just been "passed over." If it hadn't been for the blood on the doorframes, they would be dead as well. In a very real sense, they *belonged* to God. And God wanted the Israelites to remember what He had done for them.)

6. How did the people know which way to go? See Exodus 13:21, 22. Since God no longer appears in these forms, how do *you* know what paths to take in life? (We have

Scripture, the Holy Spirit, the wisdom of Christian friends, and so forth.)

7. **God didn't lead His people along the shortest route to the promised land** (13:17, 18). **Why not?** (He wanted them to avoid any major skirmishes early on.) **The next time it seems God is leading you down a roundabout path or taking too much time answering a prayer, what might you be able to assume?** (Perhaps He's trying to help us avoid some problems we don't even know about.)

8. **The Israelites were free for the first time in years. They were armed for battle** (13:18). **God was clearly with them** (13:21, 22). **So when Pharaoh changed his mind and came after them** (14:5-9), **what would you expect the Israelites to do?** Compare kids' responses with the actual actions of the Israelites in Exodus 14:10-12. **In what ways might people today choose slavery over freedom?** (Any recurring sin is a form of bondage. Only faith in Christ and ongoing obedience to God produces genuine freedom.)

9. **How did God handle the "little" problem of Pharaoh's army?** See Exodus 14:13-31. **Describe, in as much detail as possible, how you picture this incredible scene.**

10. **What's the biggest problem you're facing right now? Do you think it might be "impossible" to solve? What would you like God to do to help you? What might you be able to learn from this story?**

To help your kids put their spiritual lives in perspective, have them complete the reproducible sheet, "Graph-ic Changes." (If some of your group members haven't experienced a lot of spiritual highs and lows, ask them instead to name an amusement park ride—merry-go-round, bumper cars, tilt-a-whirl, etc. [anything other than a roller coaster]—that best illustrates their spiritual life, and explain why.) When they finish, discuss how they might be able to continue their graphs upward in the years to come. Encourage them to pursue those goals with much prayer and determination.

GRAPH-ic *changes*

As we go through life, we have our ups and downs. We may not notice the ups, and we may be too quick to whine about the downs. Just look at the Israelites. After years of slavery, they got their freedom. But as soon as they faced a problem, they were ready to give it up and go right back to Egypt— not a high point in their spiritual development.

Think about your own spiritual life. On the graph below, mark all of the high and low points you can think of; then connect the dots. Notice that a space has been left for your future. What you've done so far is past, so there's no use thinking too much about it. Better to think ahead. So when you finish your graph, list some ways to "improve your average" for your spiritual life in the days and years to come.

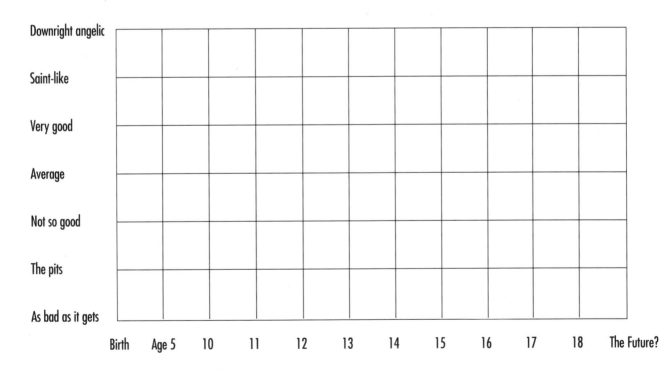

Downright angelic

Saint-like

Very good

Average

Not so good

The pits

As bad as it gets

Birth   Age 5   10   11   12   13   14   15   16   17   18   The Future?

What are some things you can do to ensure that your future is even better than your past has been?

EXODUS 15:22–17:16

Now We Blame Him for Our Food

OVERVIEW

God has just displayed His unlimited power and ability to protect His people at the Red Sea, yet the Israelites are quick to complain. Their concerns about thirst are answered in a couple of different and miraculous ways. Their fear of hunger is removed by a daily provision of manna, and their first battle is vastly successful. Yet the Israelites don't seem to be learning any lasting lessons about God's faithfulness.

OPENING ACT

(Needed: Several unusual foods and beverages)

Prior to meeting, take a trip to the supermarket to pick up a number of strange and unusual foods and beverages (smoked oysters, clam juice, mangoes, pickled anything, etc.). Then, during the meeting, conduct a "Food Dare." Remove the foods from their containers (or skins) so that group members don't have any clues as to what they are. Then assign a certain number of points for each food. The person who samples the most things (and accumulates the most points) is the winner. (Perhaps a prize of Pepto-Bismol would be appropriate.)

DATE I USED THIS SESSION _____ GROUP I USED IT WITH _____

NOTES FOR NEXT TIME _____

_____

_____

1. Think carefully. What were the last three things you complained about? Why did you complain?

2. The Israelites have just been "sprung" from slavery in Egypt. They walked through the Red Sea on dry land—after which Pharaoh's army drowned. Now that they're wonderfully free, what do you think they could possibly complain about? (It only took three days for them to give up on God again. They were thirsty and found only bitter water. So rather than ask God to do something, they immediately began to whine [15:22-24].)

3. God fixed the water, and then showed the Israelites how close they had been to a lush oasis (15:25-27). Can you think of a time when you complained a lot because something didn't go your way, yet ended up with something better instead? If so, tell us about it.

4. How would your life be different if God answered your prayers the way you wanted them answered? How do you feel about the way God answers prayers?

5. If you'd been one of the Israelites, do you think you would have believed by this time that God would take care of you? Explain. Would you have voted to take your chances in the desert or to return to Egypt and slavery (16:1-3)? (It seems that the faith of the people should be growing. Perhaps a few outspoken people were causing doubts. Sometimes we tend to "settle for" things that are familiar rather than what is best for us.)

6. How might your life be different if your faith were stronger and you were willing to take more risks for God?

7. Perhaps the miracles God had been performing seemed too random for some of the people. So when they complained about the scarcity of food, God provided a *daily* supply of bread for them (16:4-8, 17-36)—a tasty treat, at that (16:31)—along with fresh quail out of no-where (16:10-13). Do you think knowing that manna would fall from heaven each morning would have convinced you that God was nearby and watching over you?

Why or why not? (Perhaps—but the Israelites just kept grumbling [16:6-8, 20, 27].) **Why do you think the Israelites continued complaining?**

8. **Even though God had already provided sweet water from bitter, the Israelites were quick to forget the next time they got thirsty (17:1-7). Water suddenly gushing from a rock must have been an impressive miracle. Can you think of a "rocky" situation in your life from which no one but God would be able to bring something fresh? Have you been complaining about the situation or faithfully praying for something positive to happen? Why?**

9. **On their way to the promised land, the Israelites would pass through other nations. There were so many Israelites that they would be a threat—or source of revenue—for aggressive warriors. Their first battle—against the Amalekites—was further proof that God was in charge. What can you learn from Moses' battle plan (17:8-16)?** (We will face many struggles in life; our success depends on our keeping our hands upraised to God in prayer.)

10. **What's a big change you anticipate in the future? When the time comes, do you think you'll complain much about the situation? Or do you think you'll trust God to take care of things? Explain.**

Hand out copies of the reproducible sheet, "Grievance List." After a few minutes, have kids share their responses. Then say: **Go back through the list you've compiled and separate your grievances by category. Rate everything as either (1) a life-threatening problem, (2) a severe problem, or (3) an annoyance.** After group members have finished this, say: **Now add up the time segments for each category. Find out where you spend most of your time.** Explain that the Israelites should have been concerned about the battles they would face—not what was for dinner that night. Yet they seemed to lose focus on what was important. We should learn from their example to focus our concern on important areas, and not on minor irritations.

Grievance List

We all have our gripes, complaints, and concerns. Unfortunately, not many people want to listen to them. Well, here's your chance to get these things off your chest. List every single thing you can think of that

ticks you off, gets your goat,

yanks your chain, sticks in your craw,

blows your top, or gives you shivers of fright in the night.

Then, after you make your list, write an estimate next to each item you've named to indicate about how much time (on an average day) you spend thinking about, worrying about, or doing something about that particular concern.

My Gripes/Concerns List　　　　　　　　　　　**Time Estimate**

_____　　_____
_____　　_____
_____　　_____
_____　　_____
_____　　_____
_____　　_____
_____　　_____
_____　　_____
_____　　_____
_____　　_____
_____　　_____
_____　　_____
_____　　_____
_____　　_____
_____　　_____

EXODUS 18

Papa (-in-Law) Was a Rolling Business Consultant

En route from Egypt to the promised land, Moses passes close to Midian. His children, wife, and father-in-law (Jethro) come out to meet him. When Jethro sees how Moses handles conflicts among the people, he suggests a better method. After Moses learns to delegate, his work load is greatly reduced.

The reproducible sheet, "Peeble's Court," contains a number of "cases" for your kids to "try." Select kids to play the roles of prosecutors, defense attorneys, claimants, defendants, Judge Peeble, a jury (if you have a large group), and any other roles you can think of. Encourage kids to have fun with the activity. Afterward, point out that sometimes people end up spending a lot of time and money on issues that don't really matter very much. As it turns out in this session, Moses finds himself handling situations that aren't too different from the ones on the sheet—and he discovers that he needs help to keep from spending too much time on "little things."

DATE I USED THIS SESSION _____ GROUP I USED IT WITH _____

NOTES FOR NEXT TIME _____

_____

_____

1. What jobs or chores do you dislike the most? Why are those things so dreaded? Do you know of anyone else who *enjoys* doing those things? If so, who?

2. If you were Moses, leading an entire nation of people out of Egypt, through the Red Sea, into the desert where food and water were scarce, and then deep into the wilderness, what do you think would be your different jobs and responsibilities? Which would you most enjoy? Which would you least enjoy? Why?

3. Moses, following God's direction, found himself back in the same area where God had previously spoken to him from the burning bush—the place where he had met and married Zipporah. His father-in-law still lived there, so they had a family reunion (18:1-6). After dealing with a stubborn Pharaoh and a crowd of complaining Israelites, how do you think Moses felt about getting back around supportive family members? To what extent do *you* depend on family members for support and encouragement?

4. Jethro, Moses' father-in-law, hadn't been in Egypt to see God's deliverance of the Israelites. But when he heard what had happened, he worshiped God (18:7-12). **What can we learn from his example?** (We should be thankful when we see God at work in the lives of others—in addition to the things He does for us personally.)

5. The next day, Jethro saw Moses at work (18:13-16). If you'd been observing Moses, do you think you would have thought anything was wrong? If so, what suggestions might you have made?

6. What advice did Jethro offer (18:17-23)? Can you think of any organizations today that use the principle he recommended? (Many schools, businesses, missions groups, seminaries, and other organizations devote themselves to training leaders who then go out to reach more people.)

7. Moses had been getting instructions straight from God. Why should he listen to his country-bumpkin father-in-law for advice? (We can find wisdom not only from our own relationship with God, but also in the things God teaches other people. That's one reason the stories in the Bible are so important. We learn from the experiences of other people and apply those lessons to ourselves. Christian friends also may be a tremendous resource during times of need or confusion.)

8. **What did Moses think about Jethro's advice** (18:24-27)**?** (He liked it so much that he put it into practice immediately.) **Why do you think Moses hadn't done something like that on his own?** (Most of us tend to think we are better-than-average judges of people and circumstances. It's difficult to delegate power to make decisions.)

9. **The Bible doesn't really say, but what do you think might have been the result of Moses' delegating authority to other judges?** (He may have had a lot more time to do things other than settling minor disputes among people—things like writing the first five books of the Bible.)

10. **Of the "hated" chores you previously mentioned, are there any you can delegate to other people? Can you combine and share work loads with others to get jobs done faster—or at least with less disgust?**

Follow up the final question by having group members share at least one thing they could use some help with. Perhaps others in the group can provide assistance—or at least advice—for a more efficient way to get the job done. For example, if someone is having trouble with homework, another person who has no trouble in that area might volunteer to tutor. If someone is dreading a large project (house painting, farm work, etc.), perhaps some willing volunteers can be recruited (in exchange for help when *they* need it). Encourage group members to (1) be more willing to make their needs known, and (2) seek out new, and perhaps unexpected, sources of help and advice. Suggest that if Moses needed help, most of the rest of us surely do as well.

P E E B L E 'S
COURT

HELLO, AND WELCOME TO PEEBLE'S COURT—THE PLACE TO TAKE YOUR CASE when it's so lame that nobody else will even listen. Judge Harry Peeble once served as Inspector #46 for the world's largest manufacturer of left-handed guitar picks, and has been known to carry on a three-hour conversation with a "talking" clock on the "Call for the Time" line. As a result, he is perfectly suited for any job dealing with meaningless trivia—such as televised small claims court. Today he has three cases on his agenda.

Case #1: The Case of the Silent Spectator

Peter B. is an average guy who attends most of the games of his high school's team, the Mighty Muskrats. However, while the cheerleaders are cheering their little hearts out and trying to get the crowd excited about the game, Peter can frequently be seen talking to friends, eating hot dogs, or going to the rest room. Once he was even seen reading a book. The cheerleaders are taking him to court to force him to get more involved. When they scream, "Who's the greatest team of all?" they want to hear him bellow, "Muskrats! Muskrats! Muskrats!" They seek nothing other than a judge's decision to force Peter to get more involved.

Case #2: The Case of the Confiscated Clicker

Tyler and Ramona J. are brother and sister. Ramona is a couple of years older, but they have equal responsibilities around the house. Yet according to Tyler, the problem is that whenever they're watching TV, Ramona hogs the remote control. He'll be three quarters into a close football game when she walks through and clicks on a soap opera or something. Even if he gets up to change the channel, she can simply sit there and click it back. He's had enough. He's taking her to court to sue for joint custody of the clicker.

Case #3: The Case of the Too-Tough Teacher

Alan G. is a student who has recently started thinking about applying for colleges. His grades have never been very high—not because he's stupid, but because he's never applied himself very much. But now that college is on his mind, he wants to bring up his grades. His history teacher, Mr. K., recently gave him a C on a major test. Alan was really hoping to make at least a B. So he's taking Mr. K. to court. He doesn't deny that the test was graded fairly, but he's suing for mental cruelty, explaining that his grade caused him much anxiety and stress from thinking about all of the colleges he wouldn't be able to get into. He hopes the judge will rule to force Mr. K. to raise the grade.

EXODUS 19–20

God's Top Ten List

OVERVIEW

As the Israelites' journey continues toward the promised land, God calls Moses to a summit meeting on top of Mount Sinai. Due to God's presence, the entire mountain becomes holy and "off limits" to all other people. While on the mountain, Moses is given the Ten Commandments and is instructed on proper procedure for showing respect for God's holiness.

OPENING ACT

Hand out copies of the reproducible sheet, "Rush to the Finish," but don't allow anyone to look at the sheet until you give the signal. Explain that this will be a race to see who can complete his or her sheet first. (Provide a nice prize for the winner, if possible.) Emphasize that talking is prohibited during the exercise. Give a signal and let group members begin. Those who actually follow the instructions and read through the quiz before beginning will discover that all that is required of them is to write their name in the upper right corner of the page. Even so, announce that you want *everyone* to finish before determining a winner. Those who don't follow instructions will work a lot harder to eventually discover their effort has been wasted. When you get to the portion of the session dealing with the Ten Commandments, explain that the better we follow God's clear and simple instructions, the easier our lives become.

DATE I USED THIS SESSION _____ GROUP I USED IT WITH _____

NOTES FOR NEXT TIME _____

_____

_____

1. What are some things you're currently expecting from God—or at least hoping He will do for you? With all that God provides you, what are you doing for Him?

2. When the Israelites first reached Mount Sinai, God told Moses to see if they were interested in making a deal (19:3-6). **What were the terms of the agreement?** (The people of Israel would be God's "treasured possession," and He would make them special above all other nations. In return, they were to "obey [Him] fully.") **Do the terms of the agreement sound fair to you? Why or why not?**

3. The Israelites agreed to the terms (19:7, 8). **So God prepared to give them a few more specifics as to what He expected of them. How were the Israelites to prepare (19:10-15)?** (They were to wash their clothes, stay off the mountain, and abstain from sex.) **Why was this necessary?** (God's presence among them was a serious matter.)

4. **How did the people respond to the signs that God was near (19:16-19)?** (They were terrified.) **Do you have a similar response when you communicate with God? Why or why not?** (While we are told to "approach the throne of grace with confidence" [Hebrews 4:16], we should remember that God has not changed. We should always have a proper "fear" of, or reverence for, the Lord.)

5. After being sent down the mountain to warn the people to behave themselves (19:20-25), Moses returned to receive God's "top ten list" of rules for how to live. The first four (20:1-11) **had to do with the relationship between individuals and God. First and foremost was a warning about getting involved with other gods. There were a lot of idols back then. How about today?** (Anything that people put before God can be considered an idol—money, power, jobs, television, or whatever.)

6. Misusing God's name was also to be avoided (20:7). **In what ways do people misuse God's name?** (Swearing is one obvious way. But since we carry His name as "Christ"-ians, anything we do that contradicts His teaching is, in a sense, a misuse of His name. Something as "small" as breaking a promise might give others the wrong idea about the nature of the God we serve.)

7. **Keeping the Sabbath holy was another of the Ten Commandments. Do you think God has changed His mind about setting aside one day a week to do no work and honor Him instead? If not, why do you think Sunday seems like just another day to most people?** (In a secular world where so many businesses provide the same services on Sunday as on any other day, it's difficult to discipline ourselves to focus more on God for an entire day.)

8. **The last six commandments provide guidelines for better interpersonal relationships. Based on your behavior during the past week, how well would you say you've upheld Commandment #5** (20:12)**: Honoring your father and mother?**

9. **The "shall not" commandments prohibit murder, committing adultery, stealing, giving false testimony against others, and coveting what other people have** (20:13-17)**. Which of these are the easiest for you to obey? Which are hardest? Why?**

10. **Throughout the Bible, the holiness of God—His being "set apart" from sin and sinful people—is emphasized. Here we are shown that even accidentally exposing oneself to an altar devoted to God was forbidden** (20:25, 26)**. Do you think most Christians adequately understand and pay tribute to God's holiness? If so, in what ways? If not, why not?**

Some kids may think the Ten Commandments are fairly easy to follow: "No idols, no murder, no sex." To get more specific, close by reading parallel passages from Jesus' Sermon on the Mount (Matthew 5:21-30, 33-37, for example). The spirit of the law comes through much clearer. Be sure your kids go beyond legalistic compliance of the law and perceive the commandments instead as broad guidelines that point them to better relationships with God and other people.

Some tests are based on knowledge. Some are based on speed. Some are based on following instructions. This is a combination of all three. Read through the instructions below and then get started. Every second counts. **Go!**

1. Print—don't write—your name in the upper right corner of the page.

2. In the space below, write—don't print—your address and phone number. But you must use the hand you don't normally use (left hand for right-handers; right hand for lefties).

3. Without using a calculator, multiply 411 by 372. _____

4. If A = 1, B = 2, and so forth through the alphabet until Z = 26, what is the total numeric value of the letters in your first and last names?

5. Count the number of times the letter "T" is used in this sentence and write the total here: _____ .

6. Determine the number that comes next in this sequence: 1, 4, 9, 16, 25. _____

7. In the space below, write every capital letter of the alphabet that can be written using straight lines only.

8. Multiply your age by your height in inches. Subtract the total from the numeric number of this year.
_____

9. Circle the word that doesn't belong: France, Spain, Germany, Belgium, Kumquat.

10. If your grandfather's mother's sister marries your grandmother's father's son-in-law, and if they have a child, what relation will that person be to you?

11. Write down the first three words of "We Three Kings."

12. Suppose colors had different names. What you know as blue is called yellow. Your yellow is now green. Your green becomes red. And red is now called blue. What two colors would you combine to get red?

13. Determine the two whole numbers between which you would find the square root of 1,763.

14. Write down three words you would use to describe this quiz.

15. Take all of the answers for questions 2 through 14 . . . and forget about them. Complete this quiz simply by following the instructions in the first question.

EXODUS 21–31

Laying Down the Law

God begins to prepare the Israelites to become a nation. Rules for daily living are established, along with clear penalties for disobeying those rules. Plans are also laid out for building the tabernacle, as are procedures for the priests who will serve there. The people agree to be obedient. Moses and several other leaders meet God on Mount Sinai to receive His law.

Hand out copies of the reproducible sheet, "It's Your Call." Let kids work in small groups to speculate on how they might change the rules they live by. After a few minutes, collect the sheets. Read aloud some of the suggested rules or rule changes. Then, as a group, create a list of "guidelines for behavior" for your meetings—a number of rules to govern your time together. You'll also need to come up with some penalties for when the rules are broken. Try to complicate this process. For instance, one rule might be "No name calling." But if name-calling is done in jest, should it result in the same punishment as when it's done maliciously? This session deals with the importance of the law, so try to show that problems can arise when you try to live under the law.

DATE I USED THIS SESSION _____ GROUP I USED IT WITH _____

NOTES FOR NEXT TIME _____

_____

_____

1. Of all of the rules you're expected to follow at home, which one makes the least sense to you? Why? How about the rules at school? At work? At church? When a rule doesn't make sense to you, what do you do? Do you think rules are necessary? Why?

2. The Israelites had come from Egypt where, as slaves, they had to do everything they were told. Now they were completely free. So why do you think God started imposing rules on them right away? (A million people roaming through the wilderness couldn't just stumble around doing whatever came to mind. They needed some guidelines so that everyone could know what to expect. Rules can bring order out of chaos and can help guarantee everyone's rights.)

3. What was the "rule of thumb" for determining justice after an offense was committed (21:23-25)? (An equal retribution was allowed.) **Does this sound reasonable to you? Why or why not?** Point out that the intent was to prevent a vengeful person from escalating the conflict.

4. Some rules carried a death penalty for those who broke them. Why do you think a loving God would inflict such a harsh punishment? (He wanted His people to stand out from the nations around them. Anything that "dragged them down" was harshly judged.) Read Exodus 21:15, 17. **If you'd been a teenager in Israel, do you think you would have lived to see your twenties? Why or why not?** (Cursing parents was among the death-sentence offenses.)

5. Amid all of the rules and penalties was the requirement to have at least three feasts every year (23:14-19). **Why do you think these were written into the law?** (The primary purpose of the feasts was to honor God. However, God was surely aware of the people's need to rejoice and have fun.) **Do you think our church holds enough celebrations and parties? Explain.**

6. Many of the instructions given by God were in regard to building and furnishing a tabernacle, and in preparing priests to serve there. Have kids skim Exodus 25–30. **Why do you think God was so specific about these things?**

(Many of the tabernacle furnishings and priestly procedures symbolically pointed to the coming of Jesus.)

7. **Have you ever felt incompetent or out of place when people start talking about "spiritual gifts"? If so, read Exodus 31:1-11. Have you ever thought of artistic craftsmanship as a spiritual gift? In what ways might this be true today?** (Preaching and teaching are important, but the church still needs "hands-on" people who take care of the building needs, aesthetic concerns, and related matters.)

8. **"Remember the Sabbath" was one of the Ten Commandments (20:8). Now the instruction is emphasized again (23:12; 31:12-17). Why do you think the Sabbath was so important then? Do you think going to church every week is still as important today?** (There were practical reasons [23:12] as well as religious ones for the Israelites to observe the Sabbath. Today, *we* are the ones who benefit indirectly from worship and a rhythm of rest.)

9. **The Israelites agreed to follow all of the rules (24:3). Moses and some of the leaders were called up on Mount Sinai to confirm the agreement. Put yourself in the place of one of the elders. How do you think you would have felt as you witnessed the events in Exodus 24:9-18? Why?**

10. **How do you think Moses must have felt when he was handed the tablets of stone—from God Himself (31:18)? What was Moses supposed to do with them?** See Exodus 25:21.

The discussion of Old Testament rules and penalties is likely to raise questions about more current rules. If not, close by discussing any hard-to-follow rules your group members might be currently dealing with. Encourage them to start with one to three rules (either legal or spiritual) that they have trouble following. Have them write some specific goals for closer adherence to those rules. Then, at your next meeting, follow up to see how well group members are doing in achieving the goals they set.

It's Your Call

Congratulations! You've just been appointed to a new job. You are now "Person Who Revises All of the Rules Teenagers Have to Live By." Let's face it, some rules are getting a little old by now. Parents have always passed along the rules they had to live by, but times are changing. So it's up to you to

(1) Decide which of the existing rules should be thrown out completely;

(2) Decide which of the existing rules simply need to be amended a bit;

(3) Think of the things kids "get by with" because no rules exist, and create some fair rules for those situations.

For the *second* and *third* categories, decide what the penalty should be when someone breaks the rules. The decisions you make today will be used by parents, teachers, judges, and other authority figures for years to come, so be fair—and creative. (By the way, no one will know your identity, so feel free to speak your mind without any fear of recrimination from parents or peers.)

1.
RULES THAT NEED TO BE
THROWN AWAY AND
FORGOTTEN ABOUT FOREVER

2.
RULES THAT NEED
TO BE AMENDED

SUGGESTED PENALTIES

3.
RULES KIDS NEED THAT
DON'T YET EXIST

SUGGESTED PENALTIES

EXODUS 32

All That Glitters Is Not God

After Moses ascends Mount Sinai to receive the Law from God, the people begin to get restless. They convince Aaron to make them another god. Aaron makes a calf god out of the gold earrings the people brought from Egypt. When Moses returns, he sees the festive pagan celebration and gets so angry that he smashes the stone tablets God has just given him. God sends a plague on the people, but Moses intercedes to prevent Him from wiping them out completely.

Prior to the meeting, recruit one or two people as your secret accomplices. Arrange to be out of the room for several minutes at the beginning of the session. While you're gone, your accomplices should see how many people they can get to do something wrong (or unwise). Using any "tempting" materials lying around the room, what kind of trouble can your accomplices get started? When you come back in, discuss the tendency many people have to change their standards in the absence of authority. Explain the need to self-monitor our behavior so that we are just as disciplined on our own as we are when others are overseeing us.

DATE I USED THIS SESSION _____ GROUP I USED IT WITH _____

NOTES FOR NEXT TIME _____

_____

_____

1. Have you ever done something you weren't supposed to do simply because there was no one in authority around to stop you? If so, what was it? Why do you think people do things in the absence of authority figures that they would never do with supervision?

2. How long do you think you would "be good" on your own in the absence of parents, teachers, and other authority figures? Why?

3. The Israelites didn't even make it forty days with Moses gone (24:18). When they asked Aaron to make them other gods (32:1-4), why do you think he didn't refuse their request? (Perhaps he saw an opportunity for leadership and power. He was an OK guy, but we know that he was sometimes critical of Moses [Numbers 12]. Perhaps he wanted the people to like him.)

4. Why do you think Aaron built a calf, of all things? (The Egyptians had a bull-god named Apis. Perhaps Aaron was copying what he knew about other gods.) If people you know were to fashion a god, what form do you think it would take? Why?

5. To make things worse, after the golden calf was built, Aaron treated it like the real God and planned a big party (Exodus 32:5, 6). In what ways do people today try to combine Christian standards with secular practices? (The Christian observations of Christmas and Easter have become commercial opportunities for selling and secular celebration with little, if any, thought about God for many people.)

6. God saw everything that was going on and told Moses about it (32:7-10). God suggested that everyone except Moses be eliminated, so that Moses could begin fresh with a new group of people. If you had been in Moses' place, how do you think you would have replied? Why? Compare kids' responses to Moses' reply in Exodus 32:11-14.

7. Since Moses knew what was going on below before he came down the mountain, why do you think he carried the stone tablets all of the way down, only to smash them

when he got there (32:15-19)? (Sometimes hearing about something doesn't affect us as much as seeing it. Moses would have been especially sensitive to such a sinful celebration after spending the last forty days with God.) **Why do you think Moses made the people drink the ashes of the idol (32:20)?**

8. **If you had been Aaron, what would you have said when Moses asked what was going on?** Compare group members' responses to Aaron's poor excuse for a lie in Exodus 32:21-24.

9. **Apparently, even Moses' return didn't make a difference to a lot of Israelites who had shifted into "party mode." How did Moses regain control over the people (32:25-29)?** (He recruited faithful Levites to begin killing those who were "running wild.") **With three thousand people dead, do you think this punishment was too severe? Explain.**

10. **Why do you think God also inflicted a plague on the people (32:30-35)?** (Those who escaped the sword might have thought they had "gotten away" with something; the plague was a sign that God knew others were just as guilty.)

11. **If you had been Moses, do you think you would have stood up for the people—to the point of volunteering to die with them (32:30-32)? Why or why not?**

Your group members may not dance around a golden calf in defiance to God, but they are likely to be tempted by idols in other forms. The reproducible sheet, "Idol Threats," asks them to consider if the things they *say* are priorities truly are. (If the things they circle aren't also the things they designate with one or more symbols, they may have an idol problem they're not yet aware of.) Explain that *expressing* loyalty to God may be little more than empty words. Unless we back our words with time, energy, and resources, other idols may continue to influence us and consume the things we *should* be devoting to God.

Below are illustrations of a number of things that you're likely to encounter on an average day. Circle the three things that you consider to be your top priorities. (Feel free to add anything we may have left out.)

Decide which three you spend the most money on. Draw a $ sign in each of those squares.

Decide which three take most of your time. Draw a clock in those squares.

Decide which three take up most of your energy. (This can be physical, mental, or emotional energy.) Draw a lightning bolt in those three squares.

EXODUS 33–34

Take Two Tablets; Repeat If Needed

OVERVIEW

After the incident with the golden calf, the Israelites regret distancing themselves from God. But in the meantime, God and Moses appear to be closer than ever. Moses is even allowed to "see" God—at least, God's aftereffects. Then God provides Moses with another copy of the stone tablets that had been smashed. There can be no doubt that Moses has been in God's presence because of the light radiating from his face. Moses reviews what he heard from God and directs the Israelites in making the items (the tabernacle, the ark of the covenant, the lampstand, etc.) that the Lord instructed.

OPENING ACT

Instruct kids to sit in a circle. One at a time, have them give their name and favorite ice cream flavor. Each person in turn has to repeat what has already been said and then add his or her own. ("My name is Bob and I like chocolate chip." "He's Bob. He likes chocolate chip. My name is Jill and I like peppermint.") If your group is small, continue adding new bits of information one at a time: place of birth, favorite book, etc. Afterward, explain that while repetition may get monotonous from time to time, it can be an effective way to learn.

DATE I USED THIS SESSION _____ GROUP I USED IT WITH _____

NOTES FOR NEXT TIME _____

_____

_____

1. Can you think of a time when you had a fight with a friend and made up—but then found that the friendship was never quite as strong again? If so, what did you learn from the experience?

2. After the Israelites broke their covenant with God, He forgave them and agreed to keep leading them. But sin separates people from God, so God's personal presence with the Israelites would no longer be apparent (33:1-6). In what ways are people you know "stiff-necked" when it comes to spiritual things?

3. God's presence was still obvious when He met with Moses at a special tent Moses had set up (33:7-11). **Do you have a regular place to go where it seems you can get a little closer to God than usual?** If some of your group members don't have such a place, encourage them to find one.

4. What do you think it meant that God spoke to Moses "face to face" (33:11)? (In verse 20, we are told that no one can see God's face and live. But "face to face" also indicates friendship and directness. With the pillar of cloud at the entrance of the tent, no one could question the special relationship Moses had with God.)

5. Still, Moses desired to see even more of God (32:12-18). **How did God respond to his request?** See Exodus 32:19-23. **Do you ever want to see God more clearly? If so, how do you go about it? What can you learn from this passage?** (We should always try to discover more about God. Anything God doesn't want known can easily be "covered with His hand," so we never need to fear we'll see too much.)

6. Since Moses had previously destroyed the stone tablets containing the law (32:19), **God provided another copy (34:1-5, 27, 28). What attributes does God confirm about Himself as He and Moses meet again on Mount Sinai (34:6, 7)?** (Among the attributes mentioned are compassion, graciousness, slowness to anger, love, faithfulness, and forgiveness. Yet God is also just, so He must punish sin.) **Which of these attributes, if any, have you noticed in your own relationship with God lately?**

7. Do you see any contradiction in the statements that God both forgives *and* demands punishment? Explain. (Both are true. All people who trust in God for forgiveness and repent will be forgiven. But all who don't will face punishment. God's love *is* abundant, but our own stubbornness ["stiff-neck syndrome"] can prevent us from experiencing it.)

8. As the law was reviewed and rewritten by God (34:8-28), Moses wasn't tending to his physical "needs" (34:28). How do you suppose he felt? (In the presence of God where spiritual and emotional needs are met so completely, perhaps things like eating and drinking don't seem so important.)

9. The first time Moses came off Mount Sinai after forty days with God, he was shocked at the sight of the people dancing around the golden calf. This time *they* were the ones who were shocked (34:29-35). Why? (Moses' face was glowing.) Does spending time with God change *you* in any way? If so, how? If not, why not?

10. Do you relate more to Moses' relationship with God or the Israelites' relationship with God? Why? What can you learn from this session to improve your personal relationship with God?

One indication that God is "slow to anger, abounding in love and faithfulness" (34:6) was His willingness to provide another set of laws for the Israelites. Sometimes people aren't completely obedient, and God patiently forgives them. But He expects them to do better next time. The reproducible student sheet, "Written in Stone" asks kids to list several characteristics of God and then to list some things they will begin to do (or stop doing) as a result of God's characteristics. When they finish, explain that perhaps they can do better with their struggles if they follow Moses' example—spend a lot of time alone with God. It's difficult to develop spiritual depth at the mall or on the basketball court. While there is nothing wrong with such things, we need to ensure that we carve out plenty of time in our schedules to communicate with God. And like Moses, we may be surprised at the "glowing" results.

WRITTEN IN S·T·O·N·E

On the *first* tablet below, write down some of God's characteristics.

On the *second* tablet, write down some things you will begin to do—or stop doing—as a result of God's characteristics. For instance, you might write "Lord, because you are *abounding in faithfulness,* I agree to *be more faithful in my study of Your Word by setting aside at least ten minutes a day to read the Bible and pray."*

LORD, BECAUSE YOU ARE...

I AGREE TO:

LEVITICUS 1–9

Altar Egos

After receiving the Law, the proper worship of God becomes a priority for the Israelites. Various offerings are established—including burnt offerings, grain offerings, fellowship offerings, sin offerings, and guilt offerings. Consequently, the duties of the priests become much more specific. Aaron and his sons are ordained as priests, and they begin their ministry.

Hand out copies of the reproducible sheet, "Priesthood U.," to volunteers who are willing to read a part. Explain that several of the volunteers will need to ad lib their roles as instructors, attempting to envision what would be included in their "classes." The skit also contains a number of places for participants to raise questions. At the end of the skit, open up the discussion to anyone. Focus on some of the expectations for priests that group members may never have considered before.

DATE I USED THIS SESSION _____ GROUP I USED IT WITH _____

NOTES FOR NEXT TIME _____

_____

_____

1. **What is the hardest thing you have to do, physically, to worship God?** (Get out of bed on Sunday morning; get actively involved in service projects.)

2. Read Leviticus 1:1-9. **List all of the physical actions necessary for Old Testament worship.** (Selecting a perfect animal; carrying it to the tabernacle; slaughtering it; sprinkling the blood on the altar; skinning the animal; cutting it into pieces; building a fire; stacking the animal pieces [including the head and the fat]; washing the inner parts.) **What do you think would be the hardest step for you? Why?**

3. **What words come to mind when you think about this kind of worship?** (Many may think it's pretty disgusting. But these actions were not unusual for this time period. After all, dealing with blood and slaughter was necessary to fix dinner in the days before supermarkets and refrigeration.)

4. **The first chapters of Leviticus describe several kinds of offerings: burnt offerings, grain offerings, fellowship offerings, sin offerings, and guilt offerings. Why do you think there were so many?** (They served different purposes. The first three were voluntary acts of worship. The last two were mandatory after sins had been committed.)

5. **What kinds of sins do you think you'd have to commit before you needed to go to all of this effort to get forgiveness?** (Leviticus 5:1-6 indicates that even "little" things like thoughtless oaths or not speaking up when one should demanded sacrifices.) **How often do you think you'd be at the altar if we still had this type of worship today?**

6. **What if you committed a sin, but didn't have a herd and couldn't afford to buy an animal to sacrifice as commanded?** See Leviticus 5:7-13. (Other arrangements were made to accommodate the very poor. Poverty was no excuse to avoid bringing offerings to God.)

7. **Some sins required more restitution than others. For example, if someone made financial gain at another person's expense, do you think a sacrifice to God would be sufficient? Why or why not?** (Offenders *were* expected to offer a sacrifice to God, but also to reimburse the money to the victim—plus an additional twenty percent [5:14–6:7]. This was how the guilt offering differed from the sin offering, which was also mandatory.)

8. **What would happen if a lot of people decided not to make their offerings?** (Primarily, God would be displeased [which was later the case in Israel's history.] But also, since the priests were allowed to accept a portion of the offering [2:10; 7:31-34], they would suffer as well.) **Do you see any modern-day applications for us?** (Churches function as a result of people's offerings. When the money doesn't come in, they can suffer financially—and perhaps spiritually as well.)

9. Skim Leviticus 8. **A big ceremony was held to ordain Aaron and his sons as priests. Name the ways the Israelites recognized them as priests of God.** (Special dress, anointing with oil, sacrifices, a symbolic marking of their bodies with blood, a meal, and a seven-day period for them to be "set apart.") **Why do you think they made such a big fuss over the priests?** (A priest interceded before God on behalf of the people. His was more than just a "regular" job.)

10. **Do you think it was easier to be a faithful follower of God in Old Testament days or now? Why?**

Follow up the last question with a broader discussion. Certainly, we should be thankful that we don't have to go to all of the trouble to worship God that the Israelites had to. Yet we need to ask ourselves what might happen if we put more effort into our worship than we normally do. What would happen if your young people committed to Sunday morning worship in addition to their weekly meetings? Or a Bible study in addition to a fun-oriented meeting? Or an additional ten minutes of Bible reading and prayer each day? God is pleased when we volunteer our time and energy to Him (and others). Ask each group member to think of one specific commitment to "try out" for a month or so—over and above what he or she is already doing. Group members may be quite surprised at the results.

PRIESTHOOD U.

PRIESTHOOD
UNIVERSITY

ABIHU: Excuse me, sir. My name is Abihu. The registrar said I should see you.

ITHAMAR: Yes, yes. Shalom. Do come in. My name is Dr. Ithamar. I'm the dean here at Priesthood University. I understand you want to become a priest?

ABIHU: Yes, sir, I do.

ITHAMAR: What are your qualifications? You are from the tribe of Levi, I assume?

ABIHU: Of course. And I love God very much and want to help people worship Him better.

ITHAMAR: Good, good. I think you'll do just fine. Let me introduce you to some of the people who will be instructing you. *(Abihu and Ithamar begin to walk from classroom to classroom, meeting teachers.)* First, you'll be taking Slaughtering and Skinning 101. This is Mr. Mishael. Hey, Mish, tell young Abihu what he can expect in your class.

MISHAEL: *[Ad libs response.]*

ITHAMAR: Do you have any questions for Mr. Mishael? *(When finished, move on.)* This is Dr. Eleazar's classroom. He's in charge of Animal Anatomy. A good priest, you know, has to be able to reach into the carcass and grab those fatty kidneys without wasting time. You'll also need to deal with the liver, know where to slice off the tail to maximize fattiness, and so forth. Just how do you teach your students to do this, El?

ELEAZAR: *[Ad libs response.]*

ITHAMAR: Do you have any questions for Dr. Eleazar? *(When finished, move on.)* Here's our teachers' lounge. Let's see who's here. *(Enters.)* OK. This is Mr. Abijah. He'll teach you Wood Gathering and Fire Building. Mr. Benjamin is the bird specialist. He'll show you how to wring off the head, drain the blood, and tear it open by its wings. Dr. Issachar is the grain specialist. You'll have to know how to evaluate people's offerings baked in ovens or cooked in pans. You'll also have to know how to burn the offerings in the fire. Do you have any questions for these people? Or do you gentlemen have any comments? *(When finished, return to Dean's Office.)*

ITHAMAR: This is only the introductory material, you understand. Later on you'll be taught more of the special procedures—the Day of Atonement ceremony, the dress codes, and much more. I hope you're as excited to be here as we are in having you. Do you have any final questions?

LEVITICUS 11–25

Clean Living

As an example of the importance of following God's commands precisely, Leviticus 10 offers the account of Nadab and Abihu, Aaron's oldest sons, who were killed for offering "unauthorized fire before the Lord" (10:1). Leviticus 11–25 contains some miscellaneous rules and instructions for differentiating between what is "clean" and what is "unclean." Included are purification procedures, food guidelines, another mandate prohibiting eating blood, sexual prohibitions, punishments to be assigned to specific sins, and more rules for priests. The procedure for the annual Day of Atonement is also spelled out, as are other observances.

The reproducible sheet, "Restricted Diet," contains a list of various kinds of foods from which kids are supposed to select what they think would be permissible for the Israelites to eat. (Only the first item in each category would have been allowed, according to the Israelites' diet guidelines—though lemon sorbet was not likely a frequent treat for the people of Israel.) After kids guess which foods would have been OK, but before you tell them which are correct, have them read through Leviticus 11 to see for themselves how well they did. Then explain that the same clean/unclean distinctions were made in a number of areas other than food preparation.

DATE I USED THIS SESSION _____ GROUP I USED IT WITH _____

NOTES FOR NEXT TIME _____

_____

_____

1. Do you ever associate the things you eat and drink with your Christian beliefs? How about hygiene habits or illnesses? Point out that all of these things were involved in the clean/unclean distinctions for the Israelites.

2. What odd responsibilities of priests are described in Leviticus 13? (Making rulings in regard to raw flesh, boils, burns, head or chin sores, white spots, and scalp diseases leading to baldness.) How would you feel if you woke up one morning with a strange kind of skin disease—and instead of going to the doctor, your parents took you to your preacher to have you checked out?

3. How do you think the priests felt about checking to see if the hairs in infected skin had turned white or yellow, inspecting houses for mildew (13:47-59), and performing other such responsibilities? Considering both the "pros" and "cons," would you like to have been a priest in Old Testament times? Why or why not?

4. Skim Leviticus 11–15 (especially chapters 12 and 15). Who do you think would have more trouble remaining "clean": men or women? Explain. (Women automatically became unclean during menstruation or childbirth. Men became unclean due to seminal discharges [15:16], touching unclean animals [dead or alive], and other similar activities.)

5. What were the consequences for being "unclean"? How important do you think it was to the Israelites to remain "clean"? Explain. (Normal "unclean" activities such as sexual union or women's monthly periods had minimal consequences [15:16-24]. Ongoing "uncleanness" was more serious. For example, people with infectious diseases that wouldn't heal were forced to live in isolation [13:45, 46], and houses with chronic mildew were torn down and hauled away [14:43-45]. These regulations would protect the people from serious outbreaks of illness.)

6. Besides all of the "little" things done to deal with specific incidents of uncleanness, how did the Israelites deal with the *ongoing* problem of becoming unclean? (Once a year they had a very solemn ceremony called the Day of Atonement [Leviticus 16]. This was a year-to-year atonement for all of the people's sins.)

7. Sometimes we try to look for loopholes as an excuse to do things we know we shouldn't just because the prohibitions aren't "spelled out" for us. Skim through Leviticus 18. When it came to sexual activity outside of marriage, do you think God left any loopholes? What can you learn from this? (New Testament passages don't go into this degree of detail, but the demand for sexual purity is clear.)

8. Do you think you would have enjoyed being one of the Israelites? Why or why not? (Group members will probably say they wouldn't have enjoyed cleansing themselves and their clothes every time they became unclean.) If no one mentions it, point out that Leviticus 23 and 25 describe a number of feasts and celebrations for the Israelites to enjoy.

9. Leviticus 24:10-23 tells of a guy who was sentenced to be stoned because he misused God's name. Why do you think his punishment was so severe? (God was demonstrating His seriousness about the things He had proclaimed.)

10. Of all of the practices covered in this session, which ones would be hardest for you to do? Why? Which of the practices do you think should *still* be very important for us to do? Why?

The amount and nature of the content of this session may be overwhelming to your kids. (If so, imagine trying to memorize all of these rules and then live by them!) Simplify things before you close by going to the New Testament. Point out that when Jesus was asked to consider all of the laws of the Old Testament and determine which was the most important, He was able to condense everything into two simple guidelines. See if anyone knows what those guidelines are. Read Matthew 22:34-40. (Point out that "love your neighbor as yourself" comes from Leviticus 19:18.) Then spend some time brainstorming ways to make these two simple commandments more of a reality in the lives of your group members.

restricted diet

Below is a menu from Chez Monieu—one of the fanciest restaurants in the ancient Sinai Penin-sula. Let's suppose the Israelites stop by on their way to the promised land. ("The name is Moses. Reservation for 600,000 men, plus women and children.") The only problem is that the Israelites aren't allowed to eat all of the foods other people eat. Based on what you know about the Israelites' dietary restrictions, see if you can select a meal that would be OK for them to order.

Appetizers
- Crispy Insect Assortment (locusts, katy-dids, crickets, and grasshoppers)
- Fried Calamari (squid)
- Shrimp Cocktail
- Blood Sausage and Cracker Basket
- Oysters on the Half Shell

Soups/Salads
- Beef Vegetable Soup
- Camel Hump Soup
- Rabbit Stew
- Caesar Salad with Scallops

Entrées
- Lamb Chops with Garlic and Leeks
- Pork Chops with Barbecue Sauce
- Filet of Sole Stuffed with Crab

- Southern Fried Catfish
- Steak and Lobster

Sandwiches
- Hamburger
- BLT
- Bat Burger (made with real bat)
- Screech Owl on French Croissant

Desserts
- Lemon Sorbet
- Chameleon Crunch Ice Cream (with real chameleon)
- Four-and-Twenty Ravens Baked in a Pie

LEVITICUS 26

Either/Or

After having provided the Law, as well as many specifics as to how it should be obeyed and enforced, God makes clear what can be expected by those who choose to do what He commands. He is just as clear about the consequences for those who choose not to obey. It soon becomes obvious that obedience is the only wise choice—not only "because God said so," but also because adherence to God's commands results in what is best for *us*.

Call for a volunteer who is a pretty good off-the-cuff thinker and speaker. Ask him or her to talk about the *positive* aspects of a particular topic (school, a particular friend, your youth group, parents, life in general, etc.). Explain that when you give a signal (using a bell, a note on the piano, or whatever), the person should immediately switch to the opposite extreme and talk about the *negative* aspects of the topic. As you continue to signal, the person should switch back and forth between the positive and negative aspects of the topic. Let a few different volunteers give this a try. Afterward, explain that in this session, God provides two very extreme consequences for those who choose to obey Him and those who choose not to obey Him.

DATE I USED THIS SESSION _____ GROUP I USED IT WITH _____

NOTES FOR NEXT TIME _____

_____

_____

1. Suppose you have an after-school job to earn some extra money. One day, you find out that the place where you work has financial problems and can no longer pay you. If you couldn't find another job, would you consider working for no pay, just to be helpful? Why or why not?

2. Now suppose that you're expected to follow certain rules set by your parents because if you do, you get to use the car. Eventually, you buy a car of your own. Would you still follow the rules your parents have set for you? Why or why not?

3. Sometimes we tend to expect something in return for every good thing we do. When it comes to obeying God, do you think we have the right to expect anything in return? Why or why not? (We shouldn't expect it. We certainly can't earn "rights" with God. Yet God, in His grace, gives us much that we don't deserve and could never earn.)

4. Read Leviticus 26:1-5. **What good reasons can you think of to obey God if you aren't a farmer?** (Rain and harvest are promises that go beyond an agricultural level. Obedience to God results in a fruitful life—regardless of occupation.)

5. **Symbolically, how may the promises in Leviticus 26:6-8 apply to you today as well?** ("Peace in the land" might apply to peace in one's life. Removal of savage beasts may symbolize overall safety. The promise of pursuit of enemies should encourage us to be bold when we're in the minority.)

6. **What other promises can you find in Leviticus 26:9-13? How might you specifically apply them to your own life?** (God's promise to live with us and walk with us may not be as obvious as some of the others, but it is certainly one of the best things we can ever count on. In addition, He promises His favor, fruitfulness, more provision than we'll ever need, and freedom. As the Israelites were free from the yoke of Egypt, we can be free from the bondage of sin.)

7. Obeying God is our best option because His wonderful promises become reality. But there are two other options.

According to Leviticus 26:14-17, what is one of the other options? (Intentional disobedience with no remorse or repentance.) **Do you think God is waiting for us to do something wrong so He can spring into action with these punishments? Explain.** (God is patient. But if He gently shows us where we've gotten off track, and we refuse to change, He can use other methods to get our attention.)

8. **What else can happen if things begin to go bad for us and we still don't turn to God (26:18-39)?** (Little by little, the things we give priority over God—strength, jobs, health, family, possessions, other gods, emotional stability, and so forth—will be destroyed or otherwise fail to satisfy. When God comes first, He provides what we really need. But those things without God will never fulfill us.)

9. **In addition to obeying God and intentionally disobeying Him without repentance, what is the third option for responding to God's commands (26:40-46)?** (Severe disobedience for a time, with eventual confession and repentance.) **What are the results of this option?** (It's certainly better than not repenting, but it results in missing many of God's blessings. People who become Christians late in life sometimes talk about how much better their lives would have been if they had made the decision sooner.)

10. **What would you say is the "moral" of Leviticus 26?** (The sooner we become obedient to God, the better off we're going to be.) **Are you ever tempted to spin off "on your own" for just a little while to see what it's like to live without quite so much spiritual commitment? Explain.**

The reproducible sheet, "It's Your Move," contains scenarios that challenge kids to make hard decisions to be obedient. Let volunteers share what they would do in each situation. A space is also provided for kids to create a scenario of their own. If anyone wishes to read what he or she has come up with in order to get the group's response, provide time to do so. Close in prayer, asking God for the wisdom to choose to be obedient to Him, even when it is very hard to do so.

IT'S YOUR M O V E

Anyone can make good decisions when the choices are easy. But making good decisions when it costs something—well, that's a different matter. Read through the situations below and decide what you think you would do in each case. Then, at the bottom of the sheet, write down a hard decision you need to make right now. Maybe some of the other people in the group can help you with it. (They may be smarter than they look!)

1. In Sunday school, you study the parable of the good Samaritan (Luke 10:25-37). The teacher challenges you to do something specific this week to "love your neighbor as you love yourself." Well, lo and behold, that very evening as you are rushing out the door to meet your friends at the mall, your neighbor (who is about your age) calls over and stops you. She says she just wants to talk. It seems her mother has been taken to the hospital with some kind of mysterious disease, and she's been left to baby-sit with her younger brothers and sisters. You've seen her before, but she apparently goes to a different school. You think her family must belong to some Eastern religion, based on their dress and occasional strange behavior. Your friends are going to be waiting for you before they eat; then they're planning to drive around and see what's happening. So what do you do?

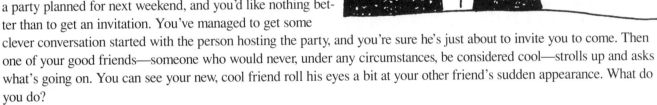

2. You're at school, where you've been getting pretty friendly with some of the cool people. You know there's a party planned for next weekend, and you'd like nothing better than to get an invitation. You've managed to get some clever conversation started with the person hosting the party, and you're sure he's just about to invite you to come. Then one of your good friends—someone who would never, under any circumstances, be considered cool—strolls up and asks what's going on. You can see your new, cool friend roll his eyes a bit at your other friend's sudden appearance. What do you do?

3. You've planned for months to go on an out-of-state summer missions trip with your youth group to help build houses for homeless people. You're also looking forward to the fun activities planned for when the missions work is over. You know your group leader is counting on a certain number of people in order to get group rates and be able to afford such a trip. But a month before you're supposed to leave, a new business in town announces it's hiring summer workers at $15 an hour—with opportunities for overtime at time-and-a-half. You know of several people from your group who have already signed up to work and are going to drop out of the missions trip. They want you to stay and work with them. To be honest, the people you're closest to are the ones who are staying. The people who are still planning to go (which is down to about half by now) are the ones you don't know very well. What do you do?

4. *Create your own scenario of a hard decision you need to make. It can be an actual situation you (or a friend) are facing, or something you make up.* _____

_____

_____

_____

NUMBERS 13–14

Land of the Giants

After God gives them some organizational and procedural instructions, the Israelites leave Sinai (but continue their whining). Miriam and Aaron begin to talk against Moses. As punishment for her opposition, Miriam contracts leprosy for seven days. When the Israelites send spies into the promised land and discover that it is inhabited by huge people, they rebel again and make plans to go back to Egypt. Joshua and Caleb, two of the spies, try to assure the people that God will lead them in triumph. But the Israelites want to stone the two spies. God tells the Israelites that, due to their lack of faith, they will have to wander in the wilderness for forty years.

(Needed: A bag of candy [optional])

Begin the session with a game of "Red Rover." Afterward, discuss how the Israelites were afraid to "come over" into the promised land, where the people were bigger. For a less active opener, give one of your larger kids a bag of candy, making it clear that the candy is for everyone. But prearrange with the person to be extremely reluctant to part with any of the candy. See how aggressively the others try to claim what you've already stated is theirs. Contrast this with the Israelites' reluctance to claim the land God said was theirs.

DATE I USED THIS SESSION _____ GROUP I USED IT WITH _____

NOTES FOR NEXT TIME _____

_____

_____

1. Have you ever tried to accomplish something significant, but failed to finish what you started? If so, why?

2. Who were Shammua, Shaphat, Igal, Palti, Gaddiel, Gaddi, Ammiel, Sethur, Nahbi, and Geuel (13:1-15)? (These were specially selected men sent to spy in the promised land. We don't remember them, however, because they advised the Israelites not to attempt to enter.) **Have you ever heard of Joshua and Caleb?** (These are known and remembered for their courage and faithfulness.)

3. God told Moses to send twelve spies into the promised land (13:1-3). **What was to be their mission?** (To explore the land and check out its people and produce.) **Of course, God already knew what the land was like. So why do you think He told Moses to send the spies?** (God had already promised the Israelites that He would deliver them safely, but perhaps He wanted them to see clearly the quality of the land He was giving them—as well as what they were up against.)

4. How did the spies' scouting expedition turn out (13:21-25)? (They returned safely and successfully after forty days.) **What might the spies have learned from their trip?** (Since God could protect twelve of His people, He could just as easily protect them all.)

5. After the spies gave contrasting reports (13:26-33), which group would you have been more likely to support? Why?

6. Were the spies supposed to recommend whether or not to move ahead? (No. The intention to enter the land had already been made clear by God.) **Then why do you suppose the ten spies advised so strongly against it?** (Many times fear prevents us from pursuing God's will for our lives.)

7. Fear can cause strange and extreme behavior. Can you think of a time when you panicked and behaved weirdly as a result? If so, what happened? How did the Israelites respond to the spies' report (14:1-10)? (They were so determined to return to Egypt [even as slaves] that they threatened to stone the ones who tried to stop them.)

8. God put a quick end to the Israelites' panicky plans (14:10). Moses pleaded on behalf of the people for God's forgiveness. But their lack of faith was not to be overlooked at this point. **What did God say the Israelites must do?** See Numbers 14:20-38. **Do you think God's judgment was too harsh? Why or why not?**

9. God's commands are important, but so is God's timing. **What happened when the Israelites decided they would enter the promised land** *after* **God told them it was too late?** See Numbers 14:39-45. **Can you think of a similar incident in your own life in which you did what you thought was right, but at what turned out to be the wrong time? If so, what happened?**

10. Joshua and Caleb took a bold stand for God. **Why do you think they had to roam the wilderness with the rest of the people who had rebelled against Moses and God?** (Sometimes God places positive influences where they can do the most good. Joshua and Caleb would eventually be rewarded, but first they were needed to help develop faithfulness among the next generation of people.)

11. It's OK to be a rebel if you're rebelling for the right reasons. Rather than going along with the crowd and rebelling against God, Joshua and Caleb rebelled against the negative mentality of the other people. **Have you ever taken a rebellious stand for what you considered a good reason? Explain.**

The reproducible sheet, "Minority Rule," lists a number of situations in which someone needs to take a stand against the crowd. Let group members determine how likely they would be to take positive action in each circumstance. Afterward, explain that if we limit our thinking to "crowd mentality," we miss out on many, many opportunities that God brings our way. Close in prayer, asking God to point out the times when we should be a bit bolder with our opinions and actions. Also ask Him for the courage to take a stand whenever we see the need to do so.

minor**i**ty
RULE

Sometimes going along with the crowd just isn't the right thing to do. There are times when people of integrity need to stand up for what's right—even if they're the only ones standing. For each of the following situations, estimate how boldly you think you would stand against the majority. (1 = Going along with the crowd, no matter what they're doing; 10 = Doing what I know is right, no matter what the crowd thinks.)

1. A new kid joins your class halfway through the school year. Your group of close friends begins making fun of him even before introductions are made.

1 2 3 4 5 6 7 8 9 10

2. A teacher nobody likes is moving this weekend and really needs some people to help. Everyone else is saying, "Yeah, right."

1 2 3 4 5 6 7 8 9 10

3. A substitute teacher will be taking over your English class for the next week. Everyone is agreeing to try to make her week as difficult as possible.

1 2 3 4 5 6 7 8 9 10

4. An overweight kid walks past your table in the cafeteria. The comments are flying: "Fatso,""Lard bottom," "Nerd," "Geek," "Dweeb." It's your turn to say something.

1 2 3 4 5 6 7 8 9 10

5. To be cool, everyone has decided to steal something from the corner grocery. It doesn't have to be big—just a candy bar or something.

1 2 3 4 5 6 7 8 9 10

6. While preparing for mid-term exams, someone comes up with a copy of the math test. Everyone is working together to solve the problems and then make "cheat sheets" for the exam.

1 2 3 4 5 6 7 8 9 10

7. A close friend of yours is active in the feminist movement. She is getting all of her friends to sign a petition advocating abortion rights. Everyone else has signed. She hands you the form and a pen.

1 2 3 4 5 6 7 8 9 10

8. You're at a party where someone has brought a joint. Everyone is taking at least one hit off it to see what it's like. It's passed to you.

1 2 3 4 5 6 7 8 9 10

9. You're driving behind an armored truck when the back door pops open and money starts flying all over the place. Other people are stuffing their pockets.

1 2 3 4 5 6 7 8 9 10

10. Other: _____

1 2 3 4 5 6 7 8 9 10

NUMBERS 20

Speak Softly; Forget the Stick

While the Israelites wander, Korah and his followers challenge Moses' authority. As punishment, they are "swallowed" by the ground. God gives Moses and Aaron instructions for how to get water in a dry place, but they seem angry at the Israelites' attitude. Moses strikes a rock instead of speaking to it, as God had instructed. As a result, Moses is told he will not enter the promised land. Later, Aaron dies. The Israelites ask permission to travel through Edom, but are turned down.

(Needed: Chalkboard and chalk or newsprint and marker)

Cut apart the pictures on the reproducible sheet, "Photo Copying." Call for volunteers, two at a time. The kids in each pair must stand back to back, with one describing the art and the other drawing it on the board. The drawer may not communicate in any way. The person describing the picture must simply describe lines, circles, and so forth. Point out how important it is to listen closely when being given instructions. Afterward, explain that Moses had problems doing exactly what God had instructed.

DATE I USED THIS SESSION _____ GROUP I USED IT WITH _____

NOTES FOR NEXT TIME _____

_____

_____

1. When was the last time a bad attitude got you into trouble? What caused your attitude? How did your attitude affect your actions? How did it affect *other* people?

2. The Israelites had a bad attitude (20:1-5). **Do you think they had a right to be angry?** (They had seen God provide water, miraculously, numerous times. He had parted the Red Sea for them. He was providing them with manna each day. He had delivered them safely to the border of the promised land, only to see their lack of faith prevent them from entering. Yet they still complained.) **What do you complain about most? Why?**

3. What did God seem to think about the people's grumbling in this case (20:6-8)? (Although God had previously suggested wiping out the people and starting over with Moses as leader, this time He was willing to act in spite of the people's negative attitudes.)

4. Once before, God had told Moses to strike a rock to get water (Exodus 17:1-7). **Why do you think He would change His instructions this time?** (Perhaps simply to show that, as God, His power is not limited to any particular method.)

5. Instead of speaking to the rock as instructed, Moses struck the rock with his staff (Numbers 20:9-11). **Why do you think he did so?** (He appeared to be fed up with the Israelites. Perhaps the sound and feel of smacking the rock was more satisfying to his emotional state than merely speaking to the rock.)

6. Why do you think water still flowed out of the rock, even though Moses disobeyed? (God had already determined to provide water. The disobedience of one of God's people doesn't prevent His will from being done for others.)

7. Apparently, Aaron had been in on the decision to strike the rock. Because of their defiance, he and Moses were denied access to the promised land (20:12). **Do you think this was a fair punishment? Why or why not?** (It seems harsh, since God had been angry with the Israelites several times before and Moses had interceded for the people. Yet Moses, more than anyone else, should have known the importance of doing exactly as God said to do.)

8. Aaron's death came relatively soon (20:22-29). Miriam, Moses' other sibling, had recently died (20:1). And Israel continued to have problems internally and in their contacts with other nations in the area (20:14-21). What do you think was Moses' emotional state during this time? (No doubt he had a lot to grieve about.) **Do you think that affected his ability as a leader? Why or why not?** (It doesn't seem to have affected his leadership abilities. He carried on faithfully. God's leaders must learn to draw strength from God during trying times.)

9. If the people had been as faithful as Moses at the edge of the promised land, they *all* could have gone in (14:5-23). Moses and Aaron were *now* going to be excluded. If you had been in Moses' place, how would you have felt? (Feelings of disappointment and perhaps even anger would be natural. Yet we need to learn from the mistakes of the past and then leave them behind us and get on with our lives.)

10. Do you think Moses' sin was going to interfere with his future relationship with God? Why or why not? (No. God would forgive him.) **What can we learn from this example?** (While we may have to live with the consequences of a previous sin, we can find full forgiveness from God and start over in a strong relationship with Him.)

Explain that Moses was "kind of" obedient when he struck the rock, but his action was still deemed sinful. Then have group members discuss some of the things they (or others their age) do that are "kind of"—but not fully—obedient to God's commands (professions of faith without church attendance, showing love toward some people while ignoring others, etc.). Close with a challenge to a more complete obedience to God—at any cost or any consequence.

PHOTO COPYING

To the Youth Group Leader:

Cut apart the following pieces of "art," but don't allow your group members to see them until you get ready to do the exercise described in the "Opening Act" section.

NUMBERS 21:4-9

Whine . . . Ouch!

Over and over again, God has shown His faithfulness to the Israelites—as well as His ability to provide for their needs. When they complained about lack of food, He gave them a daily supply of manna. Now they're complaining about the manna. So God sends poisonous snakes, which kill many of the people. The people realize their sin and plead with Moses to intercede with God. God instructs Moses to make a bronze serpent to place high on a pole where people can see it. Those who are bitten can look at the bronze serpent and be spared.

(Needed: First-aid manual, bandages, medical supplies)

Before the meeting, get a first-aid manual, bandages, and other medical supplies. Then set up various catastrophes. Enlist several kids to act as victims of a snake bite, choking, electric shock, frostbite, drowning, poisoning, and anything else from the manual that looks interesting. Lay out your "victims" around the room. Other kids should go from victim to victim, deciding how they would handle the situation if the 911 lines weren't working and if they were the only people present to help. After kids have had the opportunity to see everyone and describe what *they* would do, use the manual to determine the correct procedure in each case.

DATE I USED THIS SESSION _____ GROUP I USED IT WITH _____

NOTES FOR NEXT TIME _____

_____

_____

1. Have you ever been at an accident site where you were powerless to do anything to help the victims? If so, how did you feel? Why?

2. Suppose you come upon a scene where two cars of teenagers have crashed head-on. One car reeks of beer and marijuana while the other group looks "clean"—you even see some Bibles in the back seat. Both groups are crying out to you for help. Would you give either group preferential treatment? If so, why? If not, why not? (Most people tend to show less mercy toward people who seem to "get what they deserve.")

3. Now suppose *you* have been in an accident. Let's say you have a broken leg. Do you think you would complain about as many things the morning *after* the accident as you did the morning *before* it? Explain. (More than likely, the broken leg would become the focus of complaints for a while.)

4. Even with God providing for their every need, the Israelites had become a perpetually complaining people. What were their ongoing complaints (21:4, 5)? (Lack of pleasant living conditions, food, and water.) **Since they were in a wilderness, didn't they have the right to complain?** (God had performed miracle after miracle to get them this far. They had no reason to believe He would stop now.)

5. Have you ever done your very best to help out other people, only to hear them complain about how bad their condition still is? If so, how did you feel? How do you think God felt to hear the Israelites moan about "this miserable food"—the manna He was providing (21:5)?

6. Do you think the people were complaining just about the food or was there something deeper? (They "spoke against" God and Moses. They seem to have grown tired of their leadership, and had ceased to be satisfied with *anything*.)

7. What changed the people's attitude (21:6, 7)? (God showed them how bad things could become. He gave them just a taste of what could happen if He didn't personally oversee their safety.) **Do you think this object lesson was necessary? Why or why not?** (God had tried numerous kinds of *positive* lessons, but the people never learned.)

8. **The people had been putting down Moses. So why did they go to him when they got in trouble (21:7)?** (They knew he was close to God and could do something to help.) **If people ever put you down for being a Christian, what might you want to remember?** (If we don't allow criticism to destroy relationships, perhaps we will be appreciated by others later on.)

9. **Does the "antidote" to the snakebite threat (21:8, 9) sound like any other biblical remedy for sin? Explain.** (Jesus referred to this story as He foretold His crucifixion. [See John 3:14, 15.])

10. **Based on this story, how do you think you might reduce the amount of complaining you do?** (Perhaps it would be helpful to remember that we might face even *worse* circumstances and wish we'd appreciated how good we actually had it.)

The reproducible sheet, "Gratitude Adjustment," challenges group members to see the difference a grateful attitude can make in a number of situations. Copy the sheets and cut them in half. First, have group members complete Part 1. Then have them complete Part 2 to see if any of their answers change. Let volunteers share some of the most extreme contrasts they discover. As you wrap up the session, challenge group members to carry around a pen and paper with them for one day. They should list in one column everything they see that they should be grateful for. In a second column, they should list reasons to whine or complain. Ask them to check at the end of the day to see which column has more entries. Encourage them not to simply *list* things to be grateful for, but to actually give God the thanks He deserves for those things.

GRATITUDE ADJUSTMENT

Thank you for agreeing to this little psychological experiment. It's very simple, really. In Part 1, all we want you to do is complete these sentences as you normally would on an average day. Ready? Begin.

1. Let me tell you about my parents. Man, they really . . .

2. When I get out of bed in the morning and look at myself in the mirror, I can't help thinking . . .

3. If I could do one thing at my school without getting caught, I would . . .

4. When I think about church, I . . .

5. When I think about my life in general, the first three words that come to mind are . . .

Thank you so much for your participation. Please see your leader for Part 2.

- -

Part 2 of our experiment is much like Part 1, except that now we are releasing poisonous snakes into the room. They have been trained to zero in on negative thoughts and attack anyone who isn't being as positive as he or she possibly can be. Keeping this in mind, please complete the following sentences.

1. Let me tell you about my parents. Man, they really . . .

2. When I get out of bed in the morning and look at myself in the mirror, I can't help thinking . . .

3. If I could do one thing at my school without getting caught, I would . . .

4. When I think about church, I . . .

5. When I think about my life in general, the first three words that come to mind are . . .

Thanks again for your participation. Snakebite kits are available as you exit.

Who's the Dumb Animal Here?

As the Israelites wander through the wilderness, a king named Balak is threatened by their large numbers, so he hires a prophet named Balaam to curse them. It's clear that Balaam isn't a prophet of God, because he's after money and uses sorcery. Yet God gives Balaam instructions. When Balaam strays from what God wants him to do, an angel appears in front of him—unseen by Balaam, yet visible to his donkey. The donkey stops, and is beaten by Balaam. God opens the donkey's mouth to speak and Balaam's eyes to see, after which Balaam decides to say exactly what God tells him. So instead of cursing the Israelites, he ends up blessing them.

Play any team game your kids enjoy. Before you begin, call aside one person and tell him or her to secretly play for the opposite team. The person should be subtle, so that no one else catches on. See how long the game can go before anyone gets suspicious. Afterward, reveal your arrangement with the "traitorous" contestant. Then discuss loyalty. In this session, the topic of loyalty will keep coming up—between Balaam and Balak, Balaam and God, God and the Israelites, etc.

DATE I USED THIS SESSION _____ GROUP I USED IT WITH _____

NOTES FOR NEXT TIME _____

_____

_____

1. If animals could talk, which one would you most like to have a conversation with? Why?

2. King Balak was "terrified" (22:1-3) when he saw the large number of Israelites, even though they did nothing to threaten him. What are some things that might cause you to "fear first and ask questions later"? (A shadowy figure on a dark street? A snake in a pathway? A stranger asking directions?) Point out that while we need to maintain a certain level of suspicion, we must not allow our fear to get out of control.

3. Balak's plan was to put a curse on the Israelites to weaken them (22:4-7). What are some ways that weak people today might try to "bring down" others who threaten them in some way? (Gossip, slander, false rumors, etc.)

4. King Balak sent for Balaam to carry out the curse on the Israelites (22:7, 8). Do you think Balaam was one of God's prophets? Explain. (No. He insisted on speaking to God before acting, though he probably would have done so for any other god he was paid to consult. He received a "fee for divination," so he both worked for money and used methods forbidden to God's people [Deuteronomy 18:10-13]. Yet God still chose to speak to and through him.)

5. God replied to Balaam even though Balaam wasn't one of his prophets (Numbers 22:9-20). Do you think God still speaks to people who aren't true followers? Explain. (He certainly uses creation, conscience, His written Word, and other methods to "speak" to anyone who seeks out what He has to say.)

6. God told Balaam to go with Balak's men (22:20), but God then got angry at Balaam (22:22). How might you explain that? (One possibility is that since Balaam's *actions* were in accord with God's instructions, his attitudes or intentions must not have been.) Can you think of a time when you were doing what you were told to do, but got in trouble anyway because of a bad attitude? If so, what happened?

7. **How did God make it clear that Balaam was in trouble (22:22-35)?** (An angel of the Lord appeared in front of Balaam, but only the donkey could see him. After three encounters—and three subsequent beatings of the donkey—God first allowed the donkey to speak to Balaam and then revealed the angel.)

8. **If you were riding a donkey that suddenly turned around and began a conversation with you, what would you do? Why do you think Balaam didn't seem to be surprised by the talking mule?** (Some people suggest that since Balaam practiced sorcery [24:1], he might have been accustomed to bizarre and unnatural sights.)

9. **After his encounter with the real God, Balaam went on to meet with Balak, who gave him three opportunities to curse the Israelites. But under God's instructions, Balaam blessed them each time instead (Numbers 23–24). Balaam had learned his lesson. What lesson can _we_ learn from this?** (No matter what people set out to do to us, their power is limited by God. He can keep His people safe regardless of any evil intent of others.)

10. **When you're caught up in your own thoughts and worries, what would be a good way for God to get your attention? Try to think of a miracle on the level of Balaam's talking donkey.**

The reproducible sheet, "A Fly on the Wall," asks group members to imagine what might be "said" by animals who witness the group members' behavior on a regular basis. If volunteers wish to share what they come up with, encourage them to do so. Afterward, encourage group members to lead more consistent Christian lifestyles—even (and especially) when they are by themselves or out of sight of authority figures. Explain that faithful obedience to God should be a twenty-four-hour-a-day commitment. Challenge kids to devote more attention to the things they do with close friends or when alone.

You may have heard the saying, "I'd like to be a fly on the wall in there," referring to a room where juicy gossip is going on or weird behavior is taking place. Yes, some animals are privy to many things people try their best to keep secret from others. So suppose for a moment that the following animals could talk—like Balaam's donkey did. What might each of them say about your behavior? What tidbits or quirks would it reveal that you wouldn't really want known? Here are some examples:

• **The spider under your bed**—"Your mom cleans this room every Tuesday, so if you don't want her to see that magazine down here, you'd better move it."
• **Your best friend's cat**—"I'm going to tell my owner everything you said behind her back unless I get a case of catnip delivered to my litter box by tomorrow ."
• **The mouse beneath your sofa**—"I can't believe what you were watching on TV last night!"

A Fly on the Wall

The goldfish that sees everything that goes on in your room

The dog that tags along and observes every single thing you and your friends do outdoors

The cockroach on the dashboard of your car

The bird on the wire that overhears everything you say on the phone

The flies nesting in someone's socks in the bottom of a locker in the locker room

Wilderness Trek: The Next Generation

The men of Israel become involved in sexual immorality and idolatry with Moabite women. One man, Zimri, is even bold enough to parade his Midianite lover, Cozbi, in front of the whole assembly of Israel! Phinehas, Aaron's grandson, is so outraged by Zimri's actions that he kills Zimri and Cozbi. Moses begins to transfer his leadership responsibilities to Joshua, one of the two faithful spies who scouted the promised land. Joshua is publicly commissioned.

(Needed: Prepared slips of paper)

Put the names of your kids on individual slips of paper. Have everyone draw a slip without revealing the name on it. Then conduct a conversation in which everyone participates *as the person whose name he or she has drawn.* See how long it takes kids to identify each other based on facial expressions, body language, and use of favorite phrases. Let them see how challenging it is to "be" someone else. Afterward, compare this feeling to the way Joshua must have felt as he prepared to replace Moses as leader of the Israelites.

DATE I USED THIS SESSION _____ GROUP I USED IT WITH _____

NOTES FOR NEXT TIME _____

_____

_____

1. Who would you consider to be the greatest living leader? Why? What makes someone a good leader?

2. It was time for Moses to begin to transfer leadership of the Israelites to someone else because he was going to die soon. But God did something for Moses first. What was it (27:12-14)? (God allowed Moses to look into the promised land.) **What do you know about *your* "promised land"—heaven?** (In addition to what Jesus has told us, God has also allowed men such as Paul and the apostle John to give us some glimpses of what's in store for Christians after they die.)

3. What do you think was Moses' bigger regret: that he was going to die or that he wasn't going to get to lead the people into the promised land first? (Moses didn't seem to complain when he found out that he was going to die. He had lived a good and faithful life devoted to getting God's people out of Egypt and to the promised land. Yet perhaps he deeply regretted the sin that prevented him from seeing the end result of his life's work.)

4. If you'd been Moses, what would you have been most worried about at this point? What was Moses' biggest concern (27:15-17)? (He wanted to be sure another godly person would be appointed to continue to lead the people.)

5. Out of a group of at least 600,000 men (Exodus 12:37), why do you think Joshua was chosen? (Joshua was actually one of two who had shown the faith necessary to follow God. [See Numbers 14:6-9.] He had also spent a lot of time with Moses and in the tent of meeting where God's presence was revealed [Exodus 33:7-11]. His continued faithfulness was about to be rewarded. Also, Numbers 27:18 tells us that the Spirit was in Joshua.)

6. Why do you think the transition of power from Moses to Joshua was a gradual one (27:20)? (The Israelites had been pretty finicky about their leadership in the past and had complained a lot. It was not an easy job that Joshua was stepping into.)

7. Joshua, the replacement for Moses, was commissioned before Eleazar, the replacement for Aaron (27:18-23). A new generation is taking on great spiritual responsibility. What are some things *you* are doing to prepare for taking on spiritual responsibility in the not-so-distant future?

8. If an earthquake or tornado struck during the next board meeting of our church and killed or incapacitated the pastor and church leaders, what do you think would happen? Who would take charge? Would the church recover? If so, how long would it take?

9. Do you think there's a certain age at which people begin to get serious about assuming spiritual responsibility? If so, what is it? Is anyone ever too young to start to get involved? Is anyone ever too old? Explain.

10. What are three things you could begin to do now to help prepare for the possibility of spiritual leadership in the future?

If it doesn't come out in the last question, you might mention that one thing group members need to do is recognize and develop their God-given spiritual gifts. To help them think about this, have them fill out the reproducible sheet, "Please Pass the Muster." Let volunteers give their completed speeches to the rest of the group. Then discuss why your group members did or didn't feel convinced that they could actually lead the group if called on to do so. Explain that not everyone will become leaders, but everyone needs to find his or her role in the church and get involved. That involvement should begin *now*, not at some hazy and distant point in the future. Close with a prayer, asking God to provide the wisdom and courage needed for your young people to do whatever is expected of them in the future.

Please Pass the Muster

Congratulations! You've been nominated to run for King (or Queen) of your youth group. But you're not the only one. There's going to be an election, so you have to give a speech. We've gotten one started for you. All you need to do is fill in the blanks and then prepare to give it with all of the conviction you can muster.

Ladies, gentlemen, honored leaders, and respected members of the press:

Hello. My name is _____, but my close friends call me

_____. I am running for the coveted position of Youth Group King/Queen

because _____. Now, I know I'm not as good looking as

_____. I'm not as smart as _____. And I'm

not as psychologically disturbed as _____. But the thing that makes me

qualified for this position more than these others is _____. One thing I

think I do better than almost anyone is _____, which I can put to good use

as leader of this fine group. Of course, we all have our weaknesses, and I readily confess that one of mine

is _____.

When you think about leadership, my name might not be the first to come to mind. But I believe that the

secret to good leadership is _____. And I promise that if I'm elected, I will

never become one of those leaders who _____. Instead, I will make

_____ my top priority.

To close, I quote those famous words of _____, who said,

" _____."

DEUTERONOMY 1–3

A Look Back

The Israelites are on the verge of entering the promised land—Canaan. However, Moses won't be allowed to enter because of his disobedience at Meribah almost forty years earlier. Moses delivers a "eulogy" to the Israelites, preparing them to enter (led by Joshua) the land God promised them. Moses recalls the last forty years and the events that caused the Israelites not to be allowed to enter Canaan initially.

Use the reproducible sheet, "Jeopardonomy," to introduce Deuteronomy 1–3. Have kids work in pairs to complete the sheet. Remind kids that their answers must be in question form. (*People:* 1—Who is Moses? 2—Who is Joshua? 3—Who are Caleb and Joshua? 4—Who are Esau and Lot? 5—Who are Sihon and Og? *Divine Intervention:* 1—Who is God? 2—What is "the God of your fathers"? 3—What is anger? 4—What are "blessed . . . the work of [their] hands," "watched over [their] journey," and saw that they lacked for nothing? 5—What is "Do not be afraid of them; the Lord your God himself will fight for you"? *Potpourri:* 1—What is "Go in and take possession of [it]"? 2—What is "the Lord . . . [would] fight for [them]"? 3—What is the Lord was not with them? 4—What is forty? 5—What is "The Lord your God has given you this land to take possession of it?")

DATE I USED THIS SESSION _____ GROUP I USED IT WITH _____

NOTES FOR NEXT TIME _____

_____

_____

1. What are some geographical markers that indicate *where* Moses is speaking in the first five verses of Deuteronomy? (The Israelites are in the desert east of the Jordan River, in the Arabah.) **What are some historical markers that indicate *when* Moses is speaking?** (It's the first day of the eleventh month in the fortieth year of the Israelites' wandering. Moses is speaking after the Israelites have defeated Sihon and Og.)

2. If you had to try to "mark" today in history, how might you do it—besides just giving today's date? (Perhaps "_____ years after Communism collapsed in the Soviet Union" or "near the end of the twentieth century.") **What geographical markers might you give for the location of today's meeting?**

3. Three months after the Israelites were freed from Egyptian slavery, they received God's Ten Commandments on Mount Sinai—also called Mount Horeb. It was an exciting time; but in the second year, God instructed them to leave. Why do you think God did this (1:6-8)? (God had a lot more in store for the Israelites; He was going to lead them to the land He had promised their ancestors.)

4. Have there been times in your life where you've had to leave what you thought was a pretty good situation, but ended up in an even better one? If so, what happened?

5. When the people reached the land God had promised, what did Moses encourage them to do (1:21)? (Take possession of it without being afraid.) **Why was there no need for the people to be afraid?** (God had given them the land.) **What did the people want to do instead (1:22-25)?** (Send spies to check out what the land was like.)

6. The people started whining after the spies returned. **What were they whining about** (1:26-28)? (The inhabitants of the land were bigger and stronger than they were. The cities in the land seemed impossible to conquer.)

7. Moses tried telling the Israelites that they had no reason to whine (1:29-33). **What proof did he offer?** (The

Lord had taken care of them since they had left Egypt. He wasn't about to desert them now.)

8. **What do you think your response would have been after hearing how big the inhabitants of the promised land were and how fortified their cities were? Would you have been eager to invade? Why or why not?**

9. **How did God feel about the people's whining words and attitude?** (He was angry and vowed not to let any of the people of that generation enter the promised land.) **Why do we sometimes whine about seemingly impossible circumstances rather than simply trusting God?** (Sometimes we have a hard time seeing beyond our own abilities.)

10. **After hearing God's judgment on them, the Israelites changed their minds and tried to do what God had asked them to do in the first place** (1:40-46). **Why didn't this work?** (They were soundly defeated by the Amorites because the Lord wasn't with them.) **What lesson can we learn from this incident?** (It's important not only to obey what God commands us to do, but also to do it according to His timetable.)

(Needed: Volunteer, costume props [optional])

Bring in someone (perhaps an adult volunteer) to act as Moses. You might give the person a robe, sandals, and a fake beard to wear. Explain that you have two questions to ask Moses. Unfortunately, because Moses has been in the desert for so long, his throat is parched and he can't speak. Therefore, your kids will need to answer the questions for him. The questions are as follows: (1) "I've never seen God win any wars for me or help me conquer a promised land. Why should I obey Him?" (2) "I'll obey God when I get older. Right now, I want to have some fun. What's the problem with that?" Encourage most of your kids to offer their input in answering the questions. Ask them to give examples from Deuteronomy 1–3 to support their answers. After kids have answered both questions, close the session in prayer.

JEOPARD-ONOMY

PEOPLE	DIVINE INTERVENTION	POTPOURRI
1 His "eulogy" to the Israelites is recorded in Deuteronomy 1:1.	**1** The Israelites refused to trust Him, even though He proved Himself repeatedly (1:32).	**1** What the Israelites were to do to the land of Canaan, according to Deuteronomy 1:8.
2 This assistant of Moses was chosen to succeed Moses as leader of Israel (1:38).	**2** This name for the Lord may have been been used to remind the Israelites of His work in the past (1:21).	**2** According to Deuteronomy 1:30, this was the reason the Israelites would be able to defeat the inhabitants of the promised land.
3 Of the original generation of Israelites, they were the only two men who were allowed to enter the promised land (1:35-38).	**3** The emotion expressed by God after the people refused to trust Him (1:34-42).	**3** The reason the Israelites were defeated by the Amorites initially (1:42).
4 God instructed the Israelites not to fight the descendants of these two people (2:1-19).	**4** Three things God did for the Israelites while they were in the wilderness (2:7).	**4** The number of years that passed before Israel got a second chance to enter the promised land (1:3).
5 Two kings who were defeated by the Israelites (2:24-3:11).	**5** Moses gave Joshua this encouragement concerning Joshua's fear of the "giant nations" that lived in the promised land (3:22).	**5** Moses gave the Israelites this message after forty years in the wilderness (3:18).

DEUTERONOMY 4:1-40; 13:1-18

Idol Busters

During his second speech to the Israelites, Moses reviews the Israelites' covenant with God, as well as the blessings of fulfilling the covenant and the consequences of breaking it. He warns the people against the most dangerous joy-stealer—the worship of "counterfeit" gods and idols.

Have kids stand in a circle. Instruct them to march in place or clap their hands, creating a slow beat. One person will name a category. When he or she does, the person to his or her left must name an item in that category. The next person must then name another item in that category, and so on. For instance, if a person chooses the category "Vegetables," kids may name things like peas, corn, etc. If a person can't think of a new item, he or she is out. The next person then chooses another category. To make the game a little harder, announce that each item must be named in time with the beat. If someone misses a beat in giving a response, he or she is out. When there are just a few players remaining, you should join the game and suggest the topic "Things God Hates." Use the activity to introduce the Bible passage, in which Moses urges the Israelites to remain loyal to God.

DATE I USED THIS SESSION _____ GROUP I USED IT WITH _____

NOTES FOR NEXT TIME _____

_____

_____

Q&A

1. Deuteronomy 4:2 warns against adding to or subtracting from God's commands. What does that mean to us today? (Not only should we be careful about saying, "God says . . ." we should also be careful about accepting other people's opinions of "what God says" without first checking them against the Bible.)

2. What, according to Deuteronomy 4:5-8, separates the Israelites from other nations? (God was *near* the Israelites, so His decrees and laws were more viable than the decrees and laws of other nations' gods.) Have you ever felt especially close to God when you prayed to Him? If so, what were the circumstances? What was it like? Have you ever felt far away from God when you prayed? If so, what were the circumstances? What was it like?

3. Compare the description of Israel in Deuteronomy 4:6-8 with the way you think people describe the Christian young people in your school. In what ways might the descriptions be similar? In what ways might they be different?

4. Why is God a jealous God (4:24)? In what ways is He a consuming fire? (Since God created us, He has the right to demand total loyalty to Him. His jealousy and anger burn against all things that shift our attention from Him.)

5. Which of the promises in Deuteronomy 4:29-31 means the most to you? Why? What are some things that cause you to seek God earnestly? Explain.

6. What three groups of people does God warn against in Deuteronomy 13? (False prophets, family members or close friends, and large groups of wicked people who urge you to follow other gods.) Of course, we still have to guard against family members who would seek to lead us astray. But what about the other two groups of people—are they still around today? (Some televangelists or other leaders might be compared to false prophets. And following the lead of a large group of people—the "everyone's doing it" syndrome—is still a temptation.) Which of these people have the potential to have the most influence on you? Why?

7. How do the "false prophets" of today try to make their religion or god seem more appealing than God? (Some may offer a peaceful life with no problems. Others may offer health and wealth initiatives.)

8. Why, according to Moses, does God allow idolators to try to trick people into believing their ungodly ways (13:3, 4)? (He is testing us to see if we love Him with all of our heart and soul, and to see whether we'll keep His commands and obey Him or turn to other "gods.")

9. How might family members or close friends lead us astray or cause us to follow "idols"? (They may not deliberately try to draw us away from God. Instead, they may just draw our attention to other things.) **How might you influence your family members or close friends to follow God?**

10. How vulnerable would you say most people are to the "everyone's doing it" mentality? Explain. How aware are you of the ungodly practices and priorities of other groups of people? Do you think it's dangerous to have too much of an awareness of other people's practices and priorities? Do you think it's dangerous not to know much about other people's practices and priorities? Explain.

(Needed: Three colors of uninflated balloons, straight pins)

Hand out copies of the reproducible sheet, "Let's Bust Some Idols!" which asks kids to choose one or more of the temptation sources that are likely to affect them. Kids will tear out the appropriate coupons and exchange them for uninflated balloons and a straight pin. (You'll need to have three colors of balloons available, with each color representing one of the temptation sources.) Ask kids to name a way in which they might be tempted by the sources that were chosen; then have them blow up the balloons and tie them. After the balloons are inflated, have kids name ways in which they can resist temptation from each source or try to influence the sources positively; then have them pop the balloons. Close in prayer, asking God to give your kids strength in resisting temptation.

LET'S BUST SOME IDOLS!

Do you sometimes feel drawn away from God by what other people are doing or telling you? Don't worry, God is still with you. He just wants you to trust Him and stay loyal to Him. So go on the offensive! Choose one or more of the temptation sources below that are likely to draw your attention away from God. **Write or draw something on the paper that illustrates an example of each type of temptation in your life.** Tear out the completed coupons and exchange them for balloons. The more examples you come up with, the more balloons you get (limit three per customer). Then get ready to go on an idol-busting spree!

THIS COUPON IS GOOD FOR ONE CHANCE TO BUST AN IDOL TEMPTATION CAUSED BY **FALSE PROPHETS**

Example:

Cash value=1/100 of one cent. Offer expires today.

THIS COUPON IS GOOD FOR ONE CHANCE TO BUST AN IDOL TEMPTATION CAUSED BY **FAMILY MEMBERS OR CLOSE FRIENDS**

Example:

Cash value=1/100 of one sent. Offer perspires today.

THIS COUPON IS GOOD FOR ONE CHANCE TO BUST AN IDOL TEMPTATION CAUSED BY **POPULAR OPINION**

Example:

Cash value=1/100 of one scent. Offer retires today.

DEUTERONOMY 5; 8; 16

Forget Me Not

Moses speaks to the Israelites about their covenant with God. He recalls the experience at Mount Sinai [Horeb], highlighting the Ten Commandments and reminding the people of the fear of the Lord that they had at that time. Moses also stresses the importance of remembering God. He reviews the various annual celebrations, all of which signified various events the Israelites had experienced. Moses emphasizes that these festivals are to be both a way of remembering God and a celebration of His goodness.

Hand out copies of the reproducible sheet, "Holidaze." Give kids a few minutes to complete the sheet. (The correct answers are as follows: [1] True; [2] False—it was started by Germans who settled in Pennsylvania; [3] False—it's claimed he drove them out by beating a drum; [4] True; [5] False; [6] True; [7] False—they don't celebrate Independence Day, but they have a fourth day of July; [8] False—the tradition started in Ireland, where children carved turnips or potatoes; [9] True—but today it's celebrated on the fourth Thursday of November in the U.S. and on the second Monday of October in Canada; [10] True.) After you go through the answers, ask: **What's your favorite holiday? Why? What's your least favorite holiday? Why? Why do we celebrate holidays?**

DATE I USED THIS SESSION _____ GROUP I USED IT WITH _____

NOTES FOR NEXT TIME _____

_____

_____

1. Moses reminds the people to remember the Ten Commandments (5:1-21). **Which ones do you think people have done the best job of keeping? Which ones do you think people have done the poorest job of keeping?** (The Israelites violated several of the commandments during the golden calf incident. People today substitute many things for God.)

2. **What were the people afraid of in Deuteronomy 5:5? Why did the people think they'd die if they heard any more of God's voice** (5:25)? (Being so close to God might have made the people much more aware of their own sinfulness. Perhaps His voice was extremely powerful. This obviously was not a God to be taken lightly.)

3. **Give some examples of what it might mean to turn to the left or to the right** (5:32). **What specific things can we do to stay "on track"?**

4. Read through Deuteronomy 8. **List the things Moses is asking the people to remember.** (God's commands, God's acts of kindness, God's discipline, God Himself.) **What happens if these things are forgotten?**

5. **What causes people to forget the Lord?** (Satisfaction with life; disobedience to His commands; material things like houses and money; pride—thinking that the things we have are the result of our own efforts [8:17].)

6. **Why do you think God is so concerned about our forgetfulness?** (He knows us very well. It's obviously our nature to forget about God, especially when things are going well. The Israelites forgot Him time and time again. So do we.)

7. Read Deuteronomy 16. **Why do you think the people who put this session together wanted us also to look at this chapter? What's the connection to Deuteronomy 5 and 8?** (One of the best ways to remember God is through observing regular celebrations.)

8. **If you'd been one of the Israelites, which of the feasts do you think would have been most special to you? Why?**

9. Most Christians today don't celebrate Passover, the Feast of Weeks, or the Feast of Tabernacles. What celebrations do Christians have to help them remember God? (Regular worship services, communion, Christmas, Easter, etc.) Why are special times of celebration important?

10. What do the three celebrations in Deuteronomy 16 have in common? How are they similar to or different from contemporary religious celebrations? (Each of these celebrations involved giving something to God. Many religious holidays and gatherings today focus on what we can get out of them.)

11. Do you think most people today associate worshiping or praising God with a "celebration" atmosphere? Why or why not? What could be done in our church—or in this group—to create more of a celebration atmosphere when it comes to praising God?

Follow up the last question by giving group members an opportunity to create their own "feast of remembrance." Have group members work individually or in pairs to invent a new celebration. Using the back of the reproducible sheet, they should come up with the name of the feast, the date and time of the feast, the reason for the feast, food that would be served at the feast, and anything else we should know about the feast. Each feast should help us remember God in some way. After volunteers have shared some of their ideas, plan an actual feast, using the items suggested by your group members.

HOLIDAZE

Answer each question with a "T" for true or an "F" for false.

_____ 1. People in France celebrated New Year's Day on April 1 until the 1560s.

_____ 2. Groundhog Day began in 1869, after the editors of *The Farmer's Almanac* noted the animal's
ability to predict the weather.

_____ 3. Legend has it that Saint Patrick drove all of the snakes out of Ireland by beating them with his staff.

_____ 4. Easter most likely got its name from Eostre, the Anglo-Saxon goddess of Spring.

_____ 5. According to Hallmark Cards, more Mother's Day cards are sent than Easter cards.

_____ 6. Canadians don't celebrate a Memorial Day.

_____ 7. The British don't have a Fourth of July.

_____ 8. The practice of carving jack-o'-lanterns at Halloween is a Spanish tradition.

_____ 9. In 1863, President Abraham Lincoln declared the last Thursday in November to be the official day
of Thanksgiving in the U.S.

_____ 10. It was illegal to celebrate Christmas in Massachusetts in the late seventeenth century.

Extra Credit: My favorite holiday is _____ because . . .

DEUTERONOMY 6; 11

Love Will Keep Us Together

OVERVIEW

As Moses speaks to the Israelites who are about to enter the promised land, he cuts to the heart of the covenant between the Lord and His people. This covenant is based on God's love for His people and their love for Him. The people were to show their love for God by obeying His commands.

OPENING ACT

(Needed: Specially prepared refreshments)

Bring in treats with one ingredient left out—cookies without sugar, popcorn without salt, etc.) While kids sample the treats, hand out copies of the reproducible sheet, "The Missing Ingredient." Let kids work in small groups to complete the sheet. (The answers are as follows: [1] C—peanut butter; [2] B—Fig Newtons; [3] D—dog food; [4] F—Kellogg's Rice Krispies; [5] A—strawberry lowfat yogurt; [6] G—mayonnaise; [7] E—cling peaches baby food; [8] H—A.1. Steak Sauce.) Afterward, say: **These foods just aren't the same without the most important ingredient. In Deuteronomy 6 and 11, Moses reminds the Israelites about the most important ingredient in their relationship with God.**

DATE I USED THIS SESSION _____ GROUP I USED IT WITH _____

NOTES FOR NEXT TIME _____

_____

_____

1. Read Deuteronomy 6 and 11. **What are some of the ingredients of a healthy relationship with God mentioned in these chapters? Which one ingredient do you think is most important? Why is this ingredient so important?** (Love is the essential ingredient [6:5; 11:1, 13, 22]. All of the other ingredients, like keeping God's commands, decrees, and laws, only make sense in the context of a loving relationship. If we put the emphasis on the commands, but forget the love, we're in danger of a very empty, legalistic type of religion.)

2. Why were the Israelites encouraged to obey God in Deuteronomy 6:1-3? (So that they would enjoy long life for many years to come; so that it "may go well" with them—meaning that God would bless them.) **Do you think this applies to Christians today, or was this just for the Israelites of that time? Explain.**

3. Give some examples of loving God with all of your heart, all of your soul, and all of your strength. See Matthew 22:37.

4. According to Deuteronomy 6:6, 7, when should parents impress God's commands on their children? (When they sit at home, when they walk along the road, when they lie down, when they get up—in other words, all of the time.) **How might parents impress God's commands on their children? How well have your parents done at this? How might a kid learn about God's commands if not from his or her parents?**

5. Deuteronomy 6:8, 9 offers suggestions for remembering and doing God's commandments. What are some suggestions you might add to the list—ideas that would help *you* remember God's commands?

6. Are you more likely to "forget" God when things are going well or when things are going poorly (6:10-12)? Why? How might the things listed in Deuteronomy 6:10-12 have caused the Israelites to forget God?

7. Why was it so important for the Israelite parents to share with their kids what God had done for them (11:1-

7)? **How might sharing what God has done in your life help someone else grow in his or her faith?**

8. **What impression of God do you think you give others with your words? How about with your actions? Do you think your words and actions could cause someone else to want to begin a relationship with God? Why or why not?**

9. **Deuteronomy 11:8 says that obeying God gives us strength. How do you think this happens?** (God blesses those who obey His commands and will come to their aid when they need it.) **When was the last time you were in need of God's strength?**

10. **Name the rewards that would come to the Israelites if they observed God's commands.** See Deuteronomy 11:22-25. **Why would these rewards have been important to the Israelites?** (They were worried about trying to take over the promised land from its inhabitants.) **What blessings might God provide you as a result of obedience? Is it a "given" that those who obey will receive blessings? Explain.**

11. **Do you think that having to obey all of God's rules and commands restricts us in any way? Why or why not?**

(Needed: Post-it™ Notes)

Wrap up the session with an activity designed to help group members remember one of the key verses from this session's Bible text: Deuteronomy 6:5. Hand out Post-it™ Notes to each group member. Have kids copy the verse on the notes. Then discuss how your group members might *live* this verse. Have each group member stick one note on his or her forehead for a few minutes. Ask: **Where else could we post these notes to remind us of these things?** Give kids an opportunity to memorize the verse, so that it becomes "posted" on their hearts, where they'll always remember it. Close by reading Deuteronomy 30:15-20, a great summary of the connection between loving and obeying God. Use it to challenge your group members to make a choice for God.

The MISSING Ingredient

Listed below are the ingredients of six popular foods. However, we left out the most important ingredient of each food. First, select the missing ingredient for each food from the list below. Then guess what each food is.

1. Food:
INGREDIENTS:
_____,
SUGAR, PARTIALLY HYDRO-
GENATED VEGETABLE OILS,
SALT, MONO AND DIGLYC-
ERIDES.

2. Food:
INGREDIENTS:
_____,
SUGAR, ENRICHED WHEAT FLOUR
(CONTAINS NIACIN, REDUCED
IRON, THIAMINE MONONITRATE
[VITAMIN B1], RIBOFLAVIN [VITA-
MIN B2], CORN SYRUP, ANIMAL
OR VEGETABLE SHORTENING
[LARD OR PARTIALLY HYDRO-
GENATED SOYBEAN OIL WITH
HYDROGENATED COTTONSEED
OIL], HIGH FRUCTOSE CORN
SYRUP, WHEY, SALT, YELLOW
CORN FLOUR, BAKING SODA AND
ARTIFICIAL FLAVOR).

3. Food:
INGREDIENTS:
_____,
WATER SUFFICIENT FOR PRO-
CESSING HORSEMEAT, SOY
FLOUR, SALT, POTASSIUM CHLO-
RIDE, GUAR GUM, METHIONINE
HYDROXY ANALOGUE CALCIUM,
DL-ALPHA TOCOPHERYL ACETATE
(SOURCE OF VITAMIN E), CITRIC
ACID AND ETHOXYQUIN (PRESER-
VATIVES), MAGNESIUM OXIDE,
CHOLINE CHLORIDE, SODIUM
NITRATE (TO PROMOTE COLOR
RETENTION), IRON CARBONATE,
COPPER OXIDE, ZINC OXIDE, ETH-
YLENEDIAMINE DIHYDROIODIDE,
THIAMINE MONO-NITRATE, D-
ACTIVATED ANIMAL STEROL
(SOURCE OF VITAMIN D-3) AND
VITAMIN B-12 SUPPLEMENT.

4. Food:
INGREDIENTS:
_____,
SUGAR, SALT, CORN SYRUP,
MALT FLAVORING.

5. Food:
INGREDIENTS:
_____,
SKIM MILK, STRAWBERRIES,
SUGAR, CORN SWEETENERS,
NONFAT MILK SOLIDS, PECTIN,
NATURAL FLAVORS, AND
LEMON JUICE.

6. Food:
INGREDIENTS:
_____,
WHOLE EGGS, VINEGAR, WATER,
EGG YOLKS, SALT, SUGAR, LEM-
ON JUICE AND NATURAL FLA-
VORS. CALCIUM DISODIUM EDTA
ADDED TO PROTECT FLAVOR.

7. Food:
INGREDIENTS:
_____,
WATER NECESSARY FOR
PREPARATION AND VITAMIN C.

8. Food:
INGREDIENTS:
_____,
TOMATO PASTE, DISTILLED
VINEGAR, CORN SYRUP,
RAISINS, SALT, HERBS AND
SPICES, ORANGE BASE,
ORANGE PEEL, CARAMEL,
DEHYDRATED GARLIC, DEHY-
DRATED ONIONS.

Missing Ingredients
A. Cultured pasteurized Grade A milk **B.** Figs **C.** Golden-roasted peanuts
D. Meat by-prodcuts **E.** Peaches **F.** Rice **G.** Soybean oil **H.** Water

DEUTERONOMY 31–34

Moses' Last Hurrah

Moses gives his final "speech" to the Israelites before their entrance to the promised land—and before his death. In it, he reviews the obstacles that the Israelites will face and urges the people to maintain steady loyalty to God. He presents Joshua to the people as God's chosen leader. Moses concludes his speech by singing a song which foretells the Israelites' future rebellion against the Lord. He also specifically blesses each of the twelve tribes of Israel. Moses then climbs Mount Nebo, where God allows him to *see* the promised land. At the end of the Book of Deuteronomy, Moses dies and God buries him.

Hand out paper and pencils. Say: **You've just found out that you have a mysterious illness and have only twenty-four hours to live. Write down three things you really want to do in the next day, and three things you really want to say to the people you'll be leaving behind.** After a few minutes, collect the sheets, read them aloud, and have kids guess who wrote what. Explain that in this session, you're going to look at Moses' last few hours on earth. Throughout the Book of Deuteronomy, Moses has reminded the Israelites of things to remember before they enter the promised land—things like the importance of loving and obeying God. Now you're about to experience his final moments and hear his parting words.

DATE I USED THIS SESSION _____ GROUP I USED IT WITH _____

NOTES FOR NEXT TIME _____

_____

_____

1. Read Deuteronomy 31:1-8. **Why wasn't Moses allowed to cross over into the promised land?** See Deuteronomy 32:51. **What types of feelings do you suppose Moses had during his final hours on earth? Explain.**

2. How do you think the Israelites felt when they heard that Moses wouldn't be leading them into the promised land? How do you think they felt when they heard that Joshua would assume leadership over them?

3. How do you think Joshua felt? See Deuteronomy 31:7, 8. Without using words like "good," "happy," or "fine," how does it make you feel to know that the promise given in verse 8 applies as much to Christians today as it did to Joshua? In what specific situations would it help you to know that God will never forsake you?

4. Moses wrote down God's law and had it placed it in a special container called the ark of the covenant. Why do you think he wanted the people to read it every seven years (31:9-13)? Why not every three years, or every year? (Seven years old is about the age when children would be old enough to understand the law.)

5. God loved His people deeply, yet He knew that they would betray Him (31:16, 21). What does that tell you about God? How does it make you feel to know that God knows when you will disobey His commands?

6. God instructed Moses to write a song and teach it to the Israelites (31:19–32:47). Why? (So that after they were established in the promised land and had turned their back on God and had become corrupted by other gods, the song would testify against them.) What's the main message of the song? (God has done all sorts of great things for His people. The people will forget about Him and seek after phony gods. God will get angry and bring about justice. His ways will ultimately triumph.)

7. In Deuteronomy 33, Moses gives each tribe of Israel a blessing. If you could choose to receive one of these blessings, which one would you choose? Why?

8. **Why do you think God allowed Moses to see the promised land (34:1-4)?** (Perhaps to confirm to Moses that God would make good on His earlier promises.) **Why do you think God buried Moses in a hidden location (34:5-8)?** (Perhaps so the people wouldn't cling to the past, so they would start paying attention to their new leader.)

9. **Even though he made mistakes, Moses did great things for God (34:10-12). If you could have been in Moses' place for just one of his experiences, which one would it be? Why?**

10. **Deuteronomy 34:10-12 is an incredible epitaph for Moses. What would you want people to say about** *your* **life after you die? Why?**

11. **The New Testament quotes from Deuteronomy more than any other Old Testament book. Why do you think Deuteronomy is so widely quoted?** (Perhaps because it focuses so much on how people are supposed to live. Perhaps because it focuses on blessings God promises to His people.)

Use the reproducible sheet, "Final Exam," to review some of the key events in the life of Moses. Give group members a few minutes to complete the quiz. As you grade the quiz, have group members physically move to one of the four corners of the room (designated "a," "b," "c," and "d") to show how they answered each question. The answers are as follows: (1) b; (2) b; (3) a; (4) d; (5) a—Exodus 4:13; (6) c; (7) d; (8) d; (9) b; (10) a; (11) d; (12) c. Afterward, point out that Moses was not very confident at all when God first called him to lead the Israelites out of Egypt. (See Exodus 3–4.) But Deuteronomy 34:10-12 speaks of Moses' mighty power. Ask: **What are some of the major lessons we can learn from Moses' life?** Note how God gave Moses the skills, background, and experiences needed to be used in a mighty way. Sometimes Moses resisted, but God proved Himself trustworthy over and over. Assure your group members that if they trust in God, He will equip them to do whatever He calls them to do, whether it's something big or small.

FINAL EXAM

Moses led a pretty eventful life. Take this little test to see how much you know about some of the highlights of his 120 years. Circle the correct answers.

1. What does the name "Moses" mean?
a. "Taken from the reeds"
b. "To draw out"
c. "Mighty leader"
d. "Grandson of Pharaoh"

2. How many people did Moses murder in his lifetime?
a. None
b. One
c. Three
d. Thousands

3. Who was Moses' father-in-law?
a. Jethro
b. Jedediah (Jed)
c. Mr. Drysdale
d. Aaron

4. What did Moses do during the forty years he hid from Pharaoh?
a. He was a tent maker.
b. He wandered in the wilderness.
c. He farmed the land.
d. He tended sheep.

5. When God appeared to Moses in the burning bush and asked him to deliver the Israelites from Egypt, what did Moses say?
a. "O Lord, please send someone else to do it."
b. "O Lord, please go with me."
c. "O Lord, thank you for choosing me."
d. "O Lord, here I am. Send me."

6. Who died during the passover?
a. All of the firstborn sons of the Egyptians
b. All of the firstborn children of the Egyptians
c. All of the firstborn children and firstborn animals of the Egyptians
d. All of the children of the Egyptians

7. How did God part the Red Sea?
a. It was a trick involving mirrors.
b. The Bible doesn't say.
c. He used the power in Moses' staff.
d. He blew back the waters with a strong east wind.

8. How did Moses' father-in-law help him out?
a. He helped Moses learn to control his temper.
b. He gave Moses some advice on how to deal with his wife.
c. He lent Moses some money and cattle.
d. He gave Moses some advice on delegating responsibility.

9. What did Moses make the people do to the golden calf?
a. Hit it
b. Drink it
c. Bury it
d. Decapitate it

10. What happened after Moses saw God's "back"?
a. His face glowed.
b. His hair turned white.
c. He was blind for three days.
d. He couldn't speak for three days.

11. Why did the Israelites wander in the wilderness for forty years?
a. Because they worshiped the golden calf
b. Because they grumbled about food and water
c. Because they needed the time to get stronger
d. Because they didn't trust God to give them the promised land

12. Why was Moses prevented from entering the promised land?
a. For breaking the stone tablets in anger
b. For killing someone in anger
c. For striking a rock with his staff in anger
d. All of the above